LAST RITES

From the Track to the Scrapyard

LAST RITES

From the Track to the Scrapyard

JOHN EVANS

AMBERLEY

First published 2016

Amberley Publishing
The Hill, Stroud
Gloucestershire, GL5 4EP

www.amberley-books.com

British Library Cataloguing in Publication Data.
A catalogue record for this book is available from the British Library.

ISBN 978 1 4456 5498 0 (print)
ISBN 978 1 4456 5499 7 (ebook)

Typeset in 10pt on 13pt Sabon.
Typesetting and Origination by Amberley Publishing.
Printed in the UK.

Contents

Introduction

The factual history of the final days of Britain's old railway – the one with steam locomotives, endless branch lines and a station serving almost every village – has been written many times. In this album I am taking a much more personal approach. It is a series of essays about how the last rites were performed on the part of the railway system that my life encapsulated. This was initially Northamptonshire, which had the benefit of covering lines of three of the British Railways regions – the Western, London Midland and Eastern. Later we moved farther afield, first to Rugby, then to seaside stations on holiday and eventually on steam specials and those endless coach trips covering lots of engine sheds in a day. Do you remember them? Up at some unearthly hour and then off to about eight sheds in a day in a battered old coach with one of our party up front clutching an *Ian Allan Shed Directory* and trying to guide the hapless bus driver. We spent just long enough at each depot to get every engine number. On one of these trips I saw eight of the Western Region County class in a day, having previously never seen one. A year later they had all been withdrawn. Easy come, easy go.

If that's a summary of my last days of actually collecting engine numbers it is certainly not a reflection of the last rites of our railway in general. Those pioneers who fought with desperation to build a new railway in the nineteenth century would have been dismayed to see how quickly their hard work was cast aside. No greater example of this can be found than the old Great Central Railway. It was as if a race was on to expunge the line from a map, like taking a giant soft eraser and eliminating it in a few minutes. The Great Central was closed and much of it immediately dismantled. Only a short time after services were withdrawn south of Rugby, the track lifting team arrived. There was to be no afterthought. Much of the Great Central was instant history.

Three characters reveal themselves in these essays. Bob Mullins was a school friend who got me trainspotting again when, for some reason, my attention had moved elsewhere. We walked about a mile each way to school every day, dressed in our red-and-blue-striped blazers, coming home for lunch. He had a Hornby Dublo train set. I had a strange system devised by Tri-ang called TT – it was an idea that never worked, but they made a great streamlined Merchant Navy!

My second enthusiast partner, Bryan Jeyes, I met at Northampton College of Technology. I seem to recall getting ticked off in the library there one day by the Chief Librarian, Victor Hatley, for being 'verbally over-superheated.' He knew my passion for steam and later became a good friend. The person to whom I was chatting was Bryan, who shared many of the adventures related in these pages. He introduced me to a world outside Northampton station and shed, especially the Stratford-upon-Avon & Midland Junction Railway, a dilapidated, impoverished railway that was to become the focus of our last rites exertions in the mid-1960s. His father ran a Bedford Utilabrake van – the ultimate cool in those days. Bryan's picture of Nottingham Victoria station being demolished, which I saw for the first time only recently and is reproduced in this volume, brought a real lump to my throat.

Lastly, my brother Nick put up with my disappearance to stations while on holidays and also showed an interest, if not a passion, for railways. He accompanied me on a few shed visits and now runs the family business started back in 1937, a model shop in Northampton. A dad with a shop selling model trains – what a great way to grow up!

So this book relates a personal journey to seek out the last rites of both steam and our old-style railway. My first job was as a reporter at the local evening newspaper in Northampton, the *Chronicle and Echo*. I was privileged to be in a role where I could occasionally combine business with pleasure and could gain access to facilities not always available to other people. If this didn't work, I just used a bit of chat and hoped for the best.

I hope you enjoy reading these whimsical memories as much as I have enjoyed researching and writing them.

John Evans
Luddenden, West Yorkshire, 2015

Here is a rather feeble 'selfie' taken at Pitsford Quarries on 4 February 1966. I am opening the shed doors to take a few photos.

The Final Day ...

It was a Saturday – 25 September 1965, if I recall correctly. For most people it was just another Saturday. But for the many regulars who haunted the railways of Northampton during that poignant last summer of steam, it was a defining day.

The weather looked promising. A thin, wispy layer of cloud concealed a soft autumn sun that never quite managed to break through. I gathered my Petriflex 35 mm camera and some film and set off by bus to Far Cotton, where I would meet my pal Bryan Jeyes – and a host of others who were there to watch steam's final hours at Northampton.

This was no ordinary day. It was closure day for Northampton motive power depot – '2E' for all those who knew it well, despite the fact that a couple of years earlier it had been recoded as 1H. To enter the shed at Northampton you walked past a fairly forbidding notice warning people just like us not to enter the shed. We'd walked past it a hundred times, but this might be the last. Then we mounted the long, straggly lattice footbridge which crossed the series of tracks that formed part of the Blisworth to Peterborough line, one of the first cross-country routes to be built. It was constructed by the London & Birmingham Railway way back in 1845 and provided business for Northampton's shed, as trains often changed engines here, or worked to and from the freight yards in the south of Northampton. Once across the footbridge, you descended a set of steps next to a signal box and the shed was directly in front of you.

The odd thing about that last day was the complete lack of abnormality. Apart from the influx of visitors, it just seemed like any other Saturday morning at the shed, with engines being readied for service and loco crews wandering around doing their preparation work. We stepped off the footbridge and our feet crunched on the cinders that covered the site. We never ever entered the shed through the side door, as this was right next to the foreman's office. Although we had never been invited to leave by the shed's foreman, we always felt it best to keep a resolutely low profile. Once we reached the front of the shed, we could peer into the gloom and make out the fairly sparse number of engines stabled in its six roads. Ahead of us were a couple of Black 5s, in light steam, plus some 8F 2-8-0s and also a BR Standard 9F, No. 92087. The latter was one of three that had been moved to Northampton shed only two months earlier and we had been impressed and delighted to welcome such massive motive power to our modest collection of ex-LMS engines. Mind you, a chat with a driver a few days earlier had revealed that one of the trio, No. 92033, a refugee from the Great Central's 'Windcutter' fast freight services, was 'completely clapped out.' He was probably right, as the engine was withdrawn when Northampton shed closed.

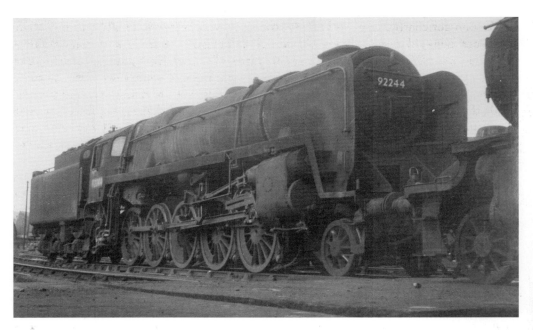

The only time I ever saw an Ebbw Junction 9F on Northampton shed was on 5 September 1965. By this time, with closure imminent, I visited the shed every night. No. 92244 had undoubtedly arrived with a train from South Wales, but usually engines were changed before Northampton. Built in 1958, she was withdrawn less than four months later with the great cull of Western Region steam.

A pleasant summer afternoon at Northampton shed sees two engines polluting the local atmosphere. On the right is scruffy Class 5 4-6-0 No. 45134 and next to it an 8F, No. 48696 (from Coalville), on 16 September 1965. Two weeks later and scenes such as this would disappear forever when the shed closed. And we would have no excuse for not starting homework early each night, rather than getting on our bikes for the thrice weekly trip to the shed.

We soon got chatting with other lads who were witnessing the shed's final hour. 'Did you hear?' one said to me, looking peevish. 'Some kid gave the shed foreman ten shillings (50p) and was allowed to pinch the number plate off 47499. Even gave 'im a spanner to get it off with.' The engine in question was one of our three resident 'Jinty' Class 3F 0-6-0 tank engines, two of which had recently been declared surplus to requirements and stored inside the shed. They had been replaced with an example of those rather peculiar LMS diesel shunters with a jackshaft drive, No. 12009, that had a very Heath Robinson form of side rods. We all loved No. 47499, which had been with us for quite a few years, so its withdrawal for scrap was particularly sad.

I looked at him quizzically. 'He bought a numberplate? Who told you that?' He shrugged his shoulders. 'Some kid.' Bob Mullins did even better – he found the pressure gauge for the same engine on the footplate in a bag and, rightly reasoning that it would not be needed again, helped himself.

When it came to shed musings, it was always 'some kid'. I walked over to where the aforementioned engine was standing, its chimney streaked with rust and its side rods removed for easy transport to the scrapyard. It was minus its front numberplate. Maybe 'some kid' really did get a prize.

'Some kid' was always ready to tell you that an unlikely engine had visited Northampton shed. In fact the most laughable tale was that a 'Clan class Pacific had once been berthed overnight at 2E.' We of course dismissed this poppycock with the disdain it deserved, until quite recently I bought a book confirming that No. 72005 *Clan MacGregor* had indeed been a visitor in September 1955.

One of our three local Jinties, No. 47286, is dumped outside the shed at Northampton on 3 September 1965. Keeping her company are Nos 41218 and 48688. The scrapyard awaits all three.

Having perused the meagre contents of the shed that Saturday, we prepared to watch the action as those engines deemed fit for further service gradually moved off shed. Most of them were not given trains to work. They headed east to the junction with the line for Northampton Castle station and the north, and set off light engine for pastures new. Eventually only two or three remained, including one of the 9Fs, No. 92087. This engine fussed around before finally heading in reverse towards the junction, and then blasting round the curve by the shed with a shriek from its whistle to head for a new life at Tyseley shed in Birmingham.

We were then aware that another engine, Black 5 No. 45190, was heading cautiously towards the turntable. Somehow we got talking to the driver, a very genial man who after a few minutes invited us on to the footplate. Can you imagine how we felt as we clambered aboard and were greeted with a smile by the young fireman? Can you imagine how all those other lads felt as they watched us up there in the cab? Well, better was to come. After a few minutes' talking, the driver, Ken Hunt, started moving the engine towards the turntable. We hesitated as if to acknowledge that we may have outstayed our welcome. 'Stay where you are,' he said. So Bryan and I became unofficial footplate visitors on No. 45190 as it was rotated on Northampton shed's turntable, the very last engine to enjoy that manoeuvre. It turned out that the crew were only getting No. 45190 ready for her next journey. We pulled up and all four of us dismounted and suitable photographs were taken. I sent the driver and fireman two colour shots each. Last year I met the fireman, Michael Hasdell, again for the first time in nearly fifty years. Coincidentally he had become a regular customer in my brother's shop in Northampton. He recalled the day very clearly and still had the pictures I had sent him. 'It was fifty-one ninety,' he said. 'Not long out of shops.' He told me that he stayed on the railways with diesels for some years, but then found a career elsewhere. Ken Hunt had retired and died some years ago.

Moving slowly along in the shed yard at Northampton on 25 September 1965 is the last engine to be prepared on shed, Class 5 No. 45190. We were on board for over an hour, much to the envy of all the other enthusiasts there that dull Saturday morning.

Here's the crew who let us share in the ceremony of the last engine to be prepared for service at Northampton shed, Black 5 No. 45190. On the left is fireman Michael Hasdell and with him driver Ken Hunt. I am still in touch with Michael, having seen him last year for the first time since 1965. Ken died some years ago.

We are in the cab of the very last locomotive to be turned on the turntable at Northampton shed (1H). This was closure day, 25 September 1965, with all the working locomotives heading north for pastures new. We were the envy of all the rail fans present!

Almost the last engine to leave Northampton shed in steam on closure date, 25 September 1965, was this 9F, No. 92087. Here she reverses past the shed before heading towards the north and a new life. She was an ex-Great Central engine.

Once No. 45190 had left the shed, a melancholy stillness descended on the proceedings. The spotters and enthusiasts quietly drifted away. For most of them it was their last visit. But I returned next day to take a few photos of the almost empty shed. Remaining inside was the breakdown train and just two engines, both withdrawn. One was Stanier 8F No. 48688 and the other was Jinty 0-6-0T No. 47499. Outside in store were our much-loved Ivatt 2-6-2T No. 41218, hero of many a speedy push-pull train to Blisworth, Wellingborough and elsewhere, and another Jinty, No. 47286.

My last visit to the shed was a month later, when I expected all the engines to have been towed away. But no, they were lined up outside the depot slowly deteriorating, although both Nos 41218 and 48688 retained their front number plates.

Maybe I should have offered the shed foreman ten shillings?

At Northampton shed (1H), which had been closed a few weeks earlier, is No. 47286 and sister engine No. 47499, both awaiting removal for scrap on 17 October 1965.

A desolate scene at Northampton shed (1H) in the autumn of 1966, a year after it closed. (Bob Mullins)

Now withdrawn, our favourite Ivatt is stored alongside Northampton shed on 23 July 1965. She had spent almost her whole life at Northampton shed, mostly speeding along with push-pull trains to Wellingborough, Bedford, Blisworth and Daventry. In the end these services all disappeared and, in need of an overhaul, she was withdrawn for scrap.

A striking photo from the top of the coaling tower at Northampton shed looking towards Bridge Street in the autumn of 1966. The power station is on the skyline, with the spur to Castle station leading off to the left. Neat rows of roofs mark the houses in Far Cotton. (Bob Mullins)

Farewell, Old Friends

It was always winter and it was always murky in scrapyards. I recently glanced through some old books showing scenes at Darlington, Airdrie, Hull and Rotherham. Symbolically, they were shrouded in mist, with small flurries of smoke rising to the sky where some once proud piece of British engineering was being reduced to chunks small enough to fit in a railway wagon. Maybe next month they would reappear as knives and forks or girders or electricity pylons. Who knows?

Our local yard at Cransley, near Kettering, appeared from nowhere. It was run by the George Cohen Group, one of a number of yards around the country to appear during this period. British Railways had always discreetly disposed of their old warhorses at their own works, but with more than a hundred steam locomotives being withdrawn each

Grange Class 4-6-0 No. 6853 *Morehampton Grange* undergoes dismantling on 20 March 1966 at Cransley. If nothing else, you can get an idea of how a firebox is constructed.

month, there simply wasn't the capacity to break up such a vast fleet of discarded assets. We discovered Cransley on a miserable early spring day which felt more like late winter. Our little group was at Kettering station and we were astonished to see a Southern H16 4-6-2 freight tank and a Q1 0-6-0 on the shed. 'Some kid' – him again – told us where to go if we wanted to see more. It was about a mile walk along a main road and there, at the old Cransley works, was a row of redundant London Underground trains.

'The last Cockfosters of them all,' wrote John Wilford, one of my *Chronicle and Echo* colleagues, using a deft turn of phrase after visiting the site.

Rather more interesting was an S15 4-6-0 and no fewer than three Schools Class 4-4-0s, all in a line and complete with smokebox number plates. It was a Saturday afternoon in March 1964 and nobody was working, so we wandered around at our leisure, seeing engines that we only knew as pictures in our Ian Allan *ABC* spotters' books. From that date onwards, we were regular visitors to Cransley. There was soon an influx of 4F 0-6-0s, then came Halls, Granges, pannier tanks and even No. 5018 *St Mawes Castle* from the Western Region. Eastern Region engines appeared too – one of the first in April 1965 was a Class 9F 2-10-0 No. 93036 from New England shed at Peterborough. This engine remained intact for several months, because suddenly there was a posse of industrial engines to provide much easier pickings. These came from the Oxfordshire Ironstone Company's quarry at Wroxton, which was most unusual in switching to diesel power. I seem to recall around ten of their little maroon steam engines were dealt with at Cransley, all arriving on low loaders by road. For a time one was set aside for possible preservation, but in the end it was cut up.

Scrapyard resident No. 47318 was a long term favourite at my home shed, Northampton (4B, then 2E and then 1H). She was transferred away in 1962, but had been at Northampton on nationalisation and was still there 14 years later. This time there will be no transfer, as she will shortly be cut up here at Cohen's yard at Cransley, near Kettering. The date is 5 March 1967.

Awaiting cutting up in the yard of George Cohen, Cransley, Northants on 5 March 1967 is Stanier 2-8-0 No. 48514. Quite a few Stanier 2-8-0s were in the yard on this day. She was a Bescot engine for a time. The connecting rod is tied on the running plate.

Class 5700 0-6-0PT No. 3607 was one of two long-time Worcester pannier tanks (the other was 3605) in the yard at Kettering on this day, 5 March 1967. Note the pre-1957 BR crest and the coupling rods still in place. She arrived from Oxley.

This Hunslet-built Jinty tank, No. 47435, was a long-term resident of Cricklewood shed in north London, but here she has made her last journey to a location still on the Midland main line, at Kettering. No. 47435 was one of three Jinties awaiting breaking up in the yard of George Cohen, Cransley, on 11 April 1967.

Here we have a 9F, which had arrived at Cohen's yard for breaking in January 1967 from Saltley shed and is seen here on 5 March 1967. She had been delivered new in 1954 and spent some time at Rugby Testing Station. Most of her career was on the Great Central. No. 92013 was not actually cut up until May.

The sight of a Southern Schools class engine was guaranteed to make a Midland spotter take breath. Here were three of them, headed by No. 30902 *Wellington*, at Cransley in March 1964 awaiting cutting up.

This is one of the early
Urie S15s, No. 30507. She
is awaiting breaking up at
Cohen's yard at Cransley,
Kettering in March 1964.
In those days engines were
delivered to scrapyards with
smokebox number plates in
place. She is surrounded by
redundant London Transport
tube stock.

This Class W 2-6-4T,
No. 31922, is standing at
Kettering by the Loddington
branch in March 1964. The
news is all bad, as the W and
Class Q1 0-6-0 No. 33013
next to her are going to the
nearby scrapyard. The smoke
is from the train on which
I am a passenger, heading for
Wellingborough. On this day
Kettering felt like it was in
the Southern Region.

Cohen's yard, Cransley,
Kettering on 4 October 1965.
The Kettering–Loddington
branch is on the left.
No. 92036 has arrived from
New England, Peterborough
and a scrap engine offers an
unusual vantage point.

Cohen's at Cransley, near Kettering, dismantled the Oxfordshire Ironstone steam fleet in late 1965 – they were replaced by some Rolls-Royce diesels. Here we see an 0-4-0ST half cut up on 26 September 1965, a gloomy Sunday.

Work is about to start on breaking up this attractive little saddle tank, which I think was part of the Oxfordshire Ironstone fleet, many of which came to Cohen's at Cransley, Kettering, for cutting up. Captured on 4 October 1965.

Another of the Oxfordshire Ironstone fleet at Kettering (Cohen's yard) awaiting scrapping on 4 October 1965. Because they were easy to cut up, these engines gave a stay of execution to some bigger engines around at this time.

Great Western 0-6-2T No. 6656 spent her last days at work with crudely stencilled numbers. Here she is, intact for the last time, at Cohen's of Cransley where she was cut up shortly after. 20 March 1966.

A shot of Stewarts and Lloyds No. 3, positioned for cutting, next to Cohen's works shunter. This is one of the Austerity-type 0-6-0STs, many of which were used by industrial lines in the post-war years.

Nothing quite touches the emotion of a railway enthusiast like a locomotive standing in front of you being cut into pieces. Sometimes they were old friends, known from their days as a living, breathing piece of carefully crafted machinery. Others were seen for the first time in a state of perilous existence, standing silently in a line awaiting their call to be next to feel that hot torch. A visit to a scrapyard was in one respect very depressing as we watched these magnificent creations being torn open, abandoned and shorn of all dignity. So why did we go? Morbid curiosity in part, but perhaps there was an element of commiseration with old friends that had fallen on the hardest of times.

Standing at Cohen's yard, Cransley on 4 October 1965 awaiting breaking up is Jinty No. 47500, an old favourite from Bletchley shed. It was always sad to see engines you knew well in the scrapyard.

Class 4 2-6-0 No. 43018 leads a line of engines at Cransley scrapyard on 5 March 1967, a grim scene. (Bryan Jeyes)

By 1969 the steam engines had all been disposed of, but then came the diesels. I paid a visit to the yard in December 1969 (winter again!) and found a Baby Deltic, No. D5906, awaiting cutting, together with some early diesel shunters. Later other diesels arrived, including some of the Western Region Hymeks. This followed the publication by British Rail of their new National Traction Plan, which basically rationalised the many classes of locomotives then in service, eliminating those types which were unsuccessful – like the Baby Deltic.

Cransley scrapyard is long gone and if you drove along the A43 today you would not realise that this minor industry was part of the landscape for many years. It's amazing to think we wandered around when it was in full swing, engines being torched in front of us and goodness knows what perils in the dust blowing in the wind. Maybe the Health and Safety people have a point …

Here we have a line-up in Cohen's yard at Cransley at the end of steam. It comprises 0-6-0ST No. 39, 0-6-0 diesel shunters 15101 and 15105 and Baby Deltic No. D5906. The date is 11 December 1969. The 0-6-0 tank may have been the last steam engine scrapped here.

Quite a few engines from the Western Region met their end in George Cohen's yard at Cransley. This pannier was one of two closely numbered 5700 tanks (3605/7) in the yard on 5 March 1967, a chilly but bright Sunday morning.

Lost in the weeds, Class 8F No. 48527 patiently awaits its fate at Cohen's yard, Kettering, in 1967.

Class 4900 4-6-0 No. 6928 *Underley Hall* stands at Cransley scrapyard on 26 September 1965, awaiting a move into the cutting zone.

Ivatt Class 2 2-6-0 No. 46519. This green engine was built at Swindon in 1952, but was about to be broken up at Kettering on 5 March 1967.

Double Jeopardy

Picture, if you will, a smoky boardroom as a group of men clutching leather briefcases find their seats and settle down to work. It is early 1948 and they are the fashionably chauvinistic members of the newly appointed British Transport Commission. At the head of the table sits Sir Cyril Hurcomb.

Hurcomb was a career civil servant who had held senior positions in the government during the difficult wartime and post-war days. Now he found himself chairing the British Transport Commission, a body created by the Labour government to oversee the smooth transition from moribund privatised companies to nationalised efficiency. Hurcomb and his team had much more than just the railways to deal with – their portfolio included docks, the former railway hotels, the railway police and museums, road haulage, many bus services and the waterways. The 1947 Transport Act had envisaged an integrated system of transport for Britain that would be much more efficient. To tackle such a massive undertaking under one umbrella was clearly unfeasible, so a series of executive bodies was charged with setting out the strategy for each division under the BTC. The Railways Executive, which basically ran British Railways, found itself with more than 20,000 steam locomotives on its hands, plus a small number of diesels, the larger of which were primarily experimental. It also controlled a railway network that had suffered greatly through the years of the Second World War. In short, the four railway companies were on their knees, both financially and operationally, due to the ravages of trying to maintain a service against all the odds from 1939 to 1945.

While the Railway Executive worked out the new standard practices it was to implement, it allowed the former companies, now gathered into six regions, to carry on very much as before. During this period, construction of steam locomotives of the company designs continued – in fact, more than 1,500 new engines were built to two dozen designs. This is 50 per cent more than the British Railways Standard types, the engines which succeeded the company designs. Among these were 341 Great Western pannier tanks, constructed in an age when it was already clear that diesel shunters were the future. Thumb through the 1948 copy of the Ian Allan *ABC* and you'll see that the LMS already had forty-five diesel shunters at work and many more on order. The Great Western, Southern and LNER each possessed a handful of shunters as well, all 0-6-0 350 bhp units that are still familiar today.

In the USA, dieselisation was well under way, and on most lines steam had fewer than ten years to live. Already the LMS had cast its eyes across the Atlantic to see what could be learned.

We tend not to see too many pictures of overseas engines awaiting their fate, but here is a wonderful 4-8-4 from the Santa Fe Railroad in the USA, owned by the California State Railroad Museum, at Sacramento on 28 April 2012. It has been standing in various locations for many years with an uncertain future, but one day it will probably be restored for display.

Against this background, it is interesting to speculate on what sort of life Robert Riddles and his team, who looked after motive power development, saw for the steam locomotive. Their decision to order no more steam shunters, save for five specialist 0-4-0 dock tanks, is significant. By 1957, most of the new Standard designs had been delivered and a brave new world, signposted by the British Transport Commission's 1954 Modernisation Plan, was about to take shape. In retrospect, the Modernisation Plan, which eventually led to the retirement of Britain's fleet of steam locomotives, was strategically sound. It failed for operational reasons. Probably the key recommendation was to replace steam with diesel and electric traction and that part of the plan was grossly mishandled. You will see in my photographs a diesel locomotive procured as part of that plan, standing in a scrapyard which only eighteen months earlier had been cutting up the steam engines it was designed to replace. With the quality and price of coal rising – especially high quality steam coal – the decision to move to diesel was understandable. Those ten years when diesels ran alongside steam, operating from the same grimy depots as steam engines and utilising mostly the same crews, were fraught for British Railways and fascinating for the enthusiast. As one of those who witnessed the first two main line diesels in regular use, Nos 10000 and 10001, I found it hard to imagine that this pair of progenitors was laying the foundations for the last rites of the railway we were witnessing. The thinking was not that new – in 1945, the Chief Mechanical Engineer of the LMS, H. G. Ivatt, had looked to

A Leicester Standard Class 2 2-6-2T was the usual motive power for the Seaton–Stamford push-pull trains. The crew of No. 84008 have disappeared for a cuppa and I've got a long wait for my train here at Seaton on 29 March 1965. This was the very last push-pull service in the country.

Only ten years old, but this baby Deltic has reached the end of the line. It awaits breaking up at Cohen's yard at Cransley on December 11 1969. A classic waste of money resulting from the poor implementation of the Modernisation Plan.

a future when diesels would replace steam and won authorisation for those two diesels. 'That forgotten day in December 1945 was really the historic instant of conception for diesel locomotives in this country,' wrote H. A. V. Bulleid.

Back at the Transport Commission, things were not going well. To order a few diesels for evaluation seems sensible – after all, the two London Midland engines and the three from the Southern (Nos 10201–3), with their English Electric engines, were giving useful experience. Yet in the late 1950s we saw diesels of many different types suddenly entering service – the frail and the feeble, the strong and the successful. Unfortunately, there were too many of the former. I do not have the 1957 Ian Allan *ABC*, but the 1959 edition lists sixteen classes of main line diesel on order or in service, with many more to come. Just think if the strategy had been right – that one or two of each class had been ordered with the promise of major purchases once thorough testing over a long time had been accomplished. The steam locomotive might well have disappeared even earlier. Maybe we should be grateful that such a convoluted way of bringing the diesels into service offered spotters and railway enthusiasts a rich variety of visual treats.

This section is entitled 'Double Jeopardy' for a reason. The failure of the Modernisation Plan to substantially reduce costs and produce a railway that could compete more effectively with the growing threat from road and air, both with freight and passenger travel, led to a second bite at a rather bitter cherry. This came in the form of the Beeching Plan, which proposed a massive reduction in the size and scope of our railway network.

But the Beeching Plan – more correctly titled 'The Reshaping of Britain's Railways' – was the second attack on the old ways, systems that included the steam locomotive.

Two Stanier 8Fs and a Standard Class 5 await movement for scrap at Newton Heath in July 1968. By this time the surviving steam had congregated in the North West. (Bob Mullins)

Entering Seaton station in Rutland is a westbound train at lunchtime on 4 June 1966. The track is weedy, but otherwise there are few clues that this is the last day of train services. In the background the lines go straight ahead to Stamford, which was the original route. The later link to Peterborough North, which this train has used, is to the right. D5036 carries a small wreath and is pulling three LMS coaches.

It is often forgotten that the hangman's noose swayed perilously over many branch and cross-country lines well before Dr Beeching wrote his prescription for the malady that inflicted Britain's Railways. In fact every year between the creation of British Railways and the start of the implementation phase of the Beeching Plan, hundreds of miles of railways were closed. Near my home in Northampton, the rambling old line from Towcester to Banbury closed to passengers in July 1951, goods trains ceasing three months later. Latterly there were two trains a day, some of them picking up only one or two passengers at the remote village stations it served. The track was taken up in 1954. Towcester, once a minor railway centre with lines heading off in four directions, suffered especially badly in the pre-Beeching era.

One of the first railway lines to lose its passenger service was that from Towcester to Olney, a delightfully bucolic journey which passed one station that was only accessible from a farm track and a very long way from civilisation. Train services started bravely on 1 December 1892, but some trains carried no passengers at all. Four months later, the passenger trains were withdrawn, never to be reinstated. Amazingly, one of the substantially built station buildings constructed for the line survives to this day as a very fine house. Possibly more astonishing is the remote Invergarry & Fort Augustus Railway, built to main line standards in Scotland and running for 24 miles. It somehow kept going until 1933, one of many lines that should never have got as far as actual construction.

The Great Northern and London & North Western Railway joint line station in its last years. Seen on 12 November 1966 is the magnificent headquarters station at Melton Mowbray North.

Blakesley station, Northamptonshire – a typical SMJ country halt. Seen here on 4 April 1966, it was demolished to make way for housing.

In many areas, the Beeching Plan simply accelerated the demise of the steam locomotive. Suddenly last rites meant not just the end of a well-loved class of steam engine, but the end of much appreciated (and little used) local railways. In my patch, around the south Midlands town of Northampton, we said goodbye to both trains and lines at the same time. Services to Blisworth and Market Harborough in January 1960 were the first to go; then passenger trains on the Bedford line followed in March 1962; lastly, in May 1964, trains to Wellingborough and Peterborough were withdrawn, this service forming part of the Beeching Plan. It meant all passenger services radiating from Northampton except those on the Euston to Rugby line disappeared. The closures robbed Northampton motive power depot of much of its traffic and, indeed, both local tank engines used for push-pull services were left with no work. One was transferred to the last push-pull service in Britain, from Seaton to Stamford, but that was also on Dr Beeching's hit list, so its stay of execution was short-lived. The other one was withdrawn.

A glance at the railway map of Northamptonshire makes dismal reading. In 1955 there were dozens of stations, most of them enjoying regular freight and passenger services. Now there are just five: Northampton, Wellingborough, Kettering, Kings Sutton and also Corby, which was reopened in 2009. It was originally closed in 1967, had a brief respite from 1987–1990 and there is now talk of half-hourly trains to London. From ashes to phoenix indeed, and a pretty lively phoenix at that, despite two performances of last rites.

Passengers no more – the end of Thrapston Bridge Street station in June 1966. This was on the line from Northampton to Peterborough, closed by Dr Beeching. (Bryan Jeyes)

With the Modernisation Plan and 'The Reshaping of Britain's Railways' to contend with, Britain's fleet of steam engines was decimated. Even attempts to save money through using diesel units were often unsuccessful. The line from Bletchley to Banbury was a pioneer in this respect, two single unit Derby-built railcars being introduced in the mid-1950s leading to a big increase in traffic. Yet the line closed in 1960. The Northampton to Bedford line also saw the use of diesel railcars, this time the small fifty-seat four-wheel units built by Park Royal. Once again they failed to save the branch, which actually reverted to steam push-pull services before closure.

Train Services – On Foot

One of the odder experiences in my railway life was a period spent walking closed railways. Of course today, with Julia Bradbury striding out along canals and abandoned tracks, walking old railways is almost a national pastime. But back in 1965, the only good reason for walking a line was being too late to take a train. My partner for these treks was Bryan Jeyes, a friend from college who seemed to be game for almost any kind of railway-based adventure. Well, actually, he suggested half of them. This included trying to restore an old Water Board beam engine with a few cans of paint and a lot of elbow grease in the hope of persuading them to preserve it. (It worked, and the engine now runs regularly at Kew Bridge Steam Museum).

One of our favourite railways was the SMJ – the Stratford-upon-Avon & Midland Junction Railway, an impecunious outfit that somehow staggered through a penniless existence for long enough to be absorbed by the LMS and then British Railways. The SMJ (Slow and Muddle Junction and the Slow, Miserable and Jolty were its nicknames) comprised a 'main line' that bobbed and weaved its weary way from Blisworth, through Towcester to Stratford-upon-Avon and on to Broom where it linked with the Midland Railway's Evesham to Redditch line. There was also the lonely section from Towcester to Olney, already mentioned, that allowed freight, including bananas, to go from Bristol to London via Evesham, Stratford, Olney and Bedford. Look at a railway map and you'll find that this is hardly the most direct way to link those two big cities. If ever there was a railway hanging in there until the last rites were duly performed, it was the SMJ.

We were much too late to travel on the line using passenger trains, which last ran in 1951 and 1952. Contemporary photos show something different from the expected solemn group of mourners. In fact the Mayor of Stratford and others in the cab of the Fowler 4F hauling the last train are smiling. This is a peculiarity of last trains – it's not unusual for them to set off accompanied by a fusillade of celebratory detonators and cheering passengers. By 1964 the freight services had called time as well, although as a lad I well remember the goods trains departing surreptitiously from the back of Blisworth station on the West Coast main line and wondering where on earth they were going. The final freight trains on the SMJ were either through trains being routed from the Great Western Main Line at Fenny Compton to Stratford and Honeybourne, or those serving local ironstone quarries at Blisworth and Byfield. So the SMJ was in final closure mode when Bryan and I started to get seriously interested in this withering survivor.

Walking old railways – this is Ravenstone Wood Junction on 29 April 1966, where the Stratford-upon-Avon and Midland Junction Railway wandered off through the trees to Towcester and Stratford. It was the start of a series of railway walks.

The huge bridge built to carry the M1 motorway over the SMJ near Roade. It was a waste of money as trains never ran beneath it. 29 April 1966.

The Great Central Railway viaduct over the SMJ at Helmdon – despite the fact that the track was removed fourteen years earlier, the SMJ track bed is in excellent condition on 19 March 1966. The viaduct stands today.

Timing is everything when walking old lines. Ideally you walk them when the track is just about to be lifted and signals, stations, signal boxes and trackside paraphernalia are still there. Next best is to walk the line when the track has gone, but the heritage has not. Our walks switched between the two. It was clearly too late to join the revellers waving farewell from the comfort of a carriage. It was also too late for those last train specials, one of which, extraordinarily, had been hauled by No. 61572, the last B12 4-6-0. With no other option available, and keen to experience the SMJ from the track, we decided to walk it all, in four or five days.

Why would anyone do this? I suppose the most interesting part of walking a railway is that you really get to know it – the stations, the scenery, the way it fits into the environment and its style. By that I mean the design of bridges, the way it twists through cuttings, clambers over embankments and the challenges the builders faced. Some of these things are not obvious, even from a slow train. But to do it on foot, you need to walk a railway before it has become completely overgrown and all the bridges removed. A glance at the SMJ's route map suggested the best bet for us would be to walk from east to west, so a long-suffering mother was persuaded to drive us to Ravenstone Wood Junction. You will have heard of Clapham Junction and probably Dovey Junction. But Ravenstone is not on most people's radar. It was situated in the middle of absolutely nowhere in rural Northamptonshire, just a signal box and some signals, with a lonely, intriguing, single track setting off through the dense trees away from the Northampton to Bedford branch line. What must it have been like to work there on a lonely winter's night, when only the odd freight train rumbled past, but otherwise with just the silence for company? At the time of our walk, in 1965, the Bedford line was closed but still in place. The SMJ had been lifted a few months earlier.

Banbury Merton Street station, end of the lines from Towcester and Bletchley. A simple and elegant overall roof, here bereft of glass, gave travellers a pleasant welcome. It was demolished many years ago. 19 March 1966.

Blisworth SMJ station on 5 April 1966, with some very nice looking Northamptonshire ironstone from Blisworth quarry awaiting movement. The old SMJ turntable pit is in the foreground – once there was a single road engine shed between the turntable and the signal box. The SMJ station behind the wagons had been converted to a parcels depot while Euston was being reconstructed.

SMJ sign near Blakesley, just after the track had been lifted on 4 April 1966.

Woodford West Junction on 4 April 1966 – the route ahead goes to Towcester while on the left is the once busy link descending to Woodford Halse. There was at one time a spur on the right to the Great Central as well.

Inside Woodford West signal box. How many men spent their days inside this box? And how sad to see their workplace about to be swept away. All the levers and instruments were still there. The only thing I took home was a black SMJ number-taker's book. It is so beautifully written with care and pride – and, obviously, back in the SMJ days this junction saw a lot of action.

Byfield station, photographed from the top of a signal post on 4 April 1966. For those who have not done this, seriously I would *not* recommend it. I did it twice – here and at Farthingstone station. Each time I felt I was going to die. Even now, fifty years later, I can feel this signal swaying when I look at this photograph.

We were encouraged by bright sunshine as we set off from Ravenstone Wood Junction. It was quite strange to think that someone, back in the 1880s, had decided that this project would be a good investment. The line eventually opened in 1891 and, like the rest of the SMJ, was a constant financial headache. Our walk showed why. The SMJ skilfully managed to avoid the few villages situated along the route. This was a country railway at its most enticing, with steep gradients and a wonderful sense of remoteness.

Our arrival at the first station, Salcey Forest, was something of a disappointment, as just the crumbling platform remained, surrounded by fields. There was no road within half a mile. Who would build a station with no road connection, yet ignore a chance to serve Piddington village about a mile further on? This was the section that enjoyed a passenger service for just four months in 1890, when some trains apparently carried no passengers at all. We walked briskly along the 10 mile route, delighting in the unspoilt farmland and lush hedgerows that persuaded at least one engine driver, according to a man I met at Northampton, to carry a shotgun on the footplate so he could enjoy rabbit for dinner later that day. Eventually we came to a huge bridge where the then new M1 motorway was built across the SMJ. It seems that the line was closed temporarily for the bridge to be built … but never reopened. Soon after, we passed through the sizeable village of Roade (no SMJ station, of course) and the huge white water tower that stood by the line. Here a lattice bridge allowed the route to cross over the West Coast Main Line, but it had been removed in 1960, so for us a detour was necessary. The removal of this bridge turned the SMJ here into two very long sidings, latterly used to store old coaches and wagons. I used to see them sometimes when we passed under an SMJ bridge as a kid and always wondered why there were trains here, but they never seemed to move.

Soon we were back on the SMJ and arriving at the second station on this 10 mile section. This was at a village called Stoke Bruerne, famous today as a canal centre, but what about in the 1890s? In those days it would have been a very small village, undoubtedly relying on the canal for passing trade at pubs and shops. The SMJ built its station in a nicely inconvenient place and they did not skimp. As at Salcey Forest, the main building was a sturdy two-storey structure and, until it closed to goods in June 1952, had a small siding. Stoke Bruerne station today remains in excellent condition. I know that a railwayman lived here for many years in its latter days as a goods depot. Today it is a very fine private house. On this day we explored inside the building, which was standing open, and then headed on the final stroll towards Towcester.

Although the track had gone, Towcester station, goods shed and signal box were intact so another voyage of exploration was made. I also drew a sketch plan of the interior of the station, which proved useful a couple of years ago when an appeal was put out by a modeller who needed to know the station's layout. He was a bit surprised to get help from California, USA (where I lived for seven years)!

With the afternoon wearing on, we still had 4 miles to cover – reversing back on ourselves for a few hundred yards and then swinging north east towards Blisworth where a connection was made with the West Coast Main Line. I can recall the sound of trains heading out of Blisworth and blasting uphill on the 1 in 71 gradient for over a mile. It wasn't exactly Shap, but it was taxing enough for a wheezy 3F or 4F 0-6-0 and, due to the sharp curve leaving Blisworth, there was no chance for a run at the gradient. About a mile from Blisworth station we saw our first signs of true railway life – the exchange sidings for Blisworth ironstone mines, which were full of wagons that had just been brought ready for filling. A bunch of saddle tanks worked the quarry, although on this day, quite late in the afternoon, all was still.

And so to Blisworth, where the SMJ had its own platform and where I had my first ride in the cab of an engine. This was where we used to go trainspotting in the 1950s and one day, having arrived on the 10.00 from Northampton Castle, we noticed an old LNWR 0-8-0 shunting in the SMJ platforms. The driver was chatty, so some of us went on the platform and were invited into the cab. A minute or so later he opened the regulator and we moved forward for a couple of hundred yards, then reversed back into the platform. A pretty good experience for an eight year old!

Our second SMJ walk a few weeks later took us back to Towcester, but a surprise was in store. The signal box was half demolished and the bridge over the main A5 trunk road was in the process of being removed. On this day we walked the 15-mile route to Banbury, much of which had been removed ten years earlier. Apart from some pretty dense undergrowth at the start of the Banbury branch, it was very easy walking and I can recall feeling that we truly had experienced what it was like to travel on this little-used line, even though it had been closed for more than a decade. At Helmdon, where the SMJ had a station (as did the Great Central – what riches the population of this little village enjoyed) we passed under the magnificent Helmdon Viaduct, which still stands. This carried the Great Central over the SMJ and the silence was broken by a northbound freight, running at its usual confident speed behind a Class 9F 2-10-0. The last few miles of this walk were on railway tracks, after the SMJ joined the line to Banbury at the delightfully named Cockley Brake Junction. Measuring your stride on sleepers has always been difficult. We also kept a good look out for trains, while assuming this section to be closed. Sometime later this was confirmed.

Three other walks allowed us to complete the whole of the SMJ, but not without some drama. The section from Towcester to Byfield was easy enough – we were clearly following the track-lifting gang very closely as signals and other lineside features were still in place. Eventually we were walking along the tracks. At Byfield station I clambered to the top of a signal post to get a nice general photograph of the station. I only did this twice in my life and I have to say it was a very scary experience, and pretty stupid.

The next section from Byfield onwards included the connection to Byfield Ironstone Quarry, where we found an 0-6-0ST saddle tank stranded on a short piece of track, the rest of the site devoid of rails. Recommencing at Byfield station, we did well until near Fenny Compton. Here a bridge over the canal had recently been removed near the Great Western main line, resulting in a lengthy diversion. The sight of a 9F or two heading through the pretty countryside was some compensation. There followed a walk back to the SMJ over a field full of distinctly aggressive cows, which blocked our way through a bridge under the GWR line. Eventually we clambered up on to the SMJ and were rewarded by the passing of the Up Birmingham Pullman in its striking 'Nanking' blue livery and in many ways the forerunner of today's High Speed Trains and other express diesel multiple units.

Fenny Compton was the scene of some last minute investment in the SMJ. It was decided to route freights, which had previously gone through Banbury and Swindon, along the SMJ to Stratford, where a new spur was built in 1960 linking the station with

The 0-6-0ST *Cherwell* at Byfield Mines on 23 June 1966. She ended up going to New Street Recreation Ground in Daventry as a children's plaything, but was saved in 2001 by the Rushden Transport Museum. In my picture she is isolated on a short piece of track.

the Great Western line to Honeybourne and Cheltenham. At Fenny station, we watched trains for a while and then set off along the tracks towards Stratford, planning to end our walk at Kineton station. We were destined not to reach it. Marching confidently along the tracks, we came under a bridge and saw the large military camp at Kineton to our left. We were a bit surprised to see this, not having any idea that there was a vast munitions depot here. Not only that, but it appeared they had suffered something of an accident – a railway wagon in one of the sidings was off the rails. We trudged on, but were soon hailed by two men in military uniform. We were asked how we had managed to enter a top security base and innocently replied we were just walking an old railway line. This answer was not well received, especially as we had cameras, and we were arrested and whisked off to a small room for interrogation. By this time, Bryan and I had realised these soldiers were military policemen. After a bit of time being questioned and assuring them we had not been photographing the camp, we were allowed to go, but instead of being sent back to the SMJ, we were escorted out of the main entrance. A long walk ensued as we tried to get to a village, but look at a map and you'll see there is not much civilisation around. Eventually we reached a main road and caught a bus to Banbury, from where we somehow made our way back to Northampton. Quite how is lost in the mists of time.

Railway walks sometimes allowed views of working steam – waiting at a signal at Fenny Compton on 23 June 1966 is Class 9F 2-10-0 No. 92247. She is heading an iron ore train travelling north. Although the Western Region eliminated steam in 1965, parts of the old GWR system – such as here – were moved to the London Midland Region and still saw some steam. This 9F is one of a fleet of ex-Western Region engines then based at Banbury shed.

The Kineton Ministry of Defence depot on 23 June 1966, showing the layout then in use. At the time this and the section from Blisworth to Blisworth Mines were all that remained in use of the old SMJ. Trouble was ahead for Bryan and me.

Kineton Ministry of Defence depot on 23 June 1966, scene of our arrest while walking the SMJ. Who said being a railway enthusiast was boring? A small mishap is being cleared up.

Stratford Old Town station, headquarters of the SMJ, pictured on 30 August 1966 on a very wet day. The new, but already abandoned, south spur heads away to the left. Curving slightly to the right is the way ahead to Broom, which had closed in 1960. A bad weather day for paying our last respects to the SMJ.

Somewhat shaken by this experience, it was a few weeks before we ventured out again to complete the walk from Kineton (station – not the military camp!). This was a miserable experience as it rained all day. Stratford Old Town station, the headquarters of the SMJ, was in the first stages of being demolished. We trudged on, only the sight of a long row of derelict Fowler ploughing engines spicing up the walk. I can remember that we gave up the struggle a short distance from Broom, the proposed end of our trail, and also the end of the SMJ. Eventually we reached this station on a sunny Sunday a few weeks later, courtesy of another ride from parents.

We also walked the railways from Buckingham to Banbury and much of the Northampton to Wellingborough route. But nothing came close to really getting to know the old SMJ. Those notes and the colour pictures I took have helped one or two authors with their books, as on returning home each time I wrote a detailed description of the route (in true teenager, anorak style!). Somehow that old maroon writing book has survived over many years, as has an SMJ number-taker's book listing trains passing in 1922. I rescued this from some rubbish on the floor of Woodford West signal box, which was destroyed a few days later. It's very interesting, despite being in poor condition. On 22 September 1922 it shows a train running from Penmaenmawr in North Wales on its way to Princes Risborough passing the box. From Byfield signal box I found a rule book with the name 'W. J. Steel, Byfield' very neatly written in it. Lastly, I have a small 'Private' sign from Towcester station. As the site is now a Tesco supermarket, having also been an

At Binton station, on 12 May 1966, we had a very unusual encounter with rows of old Fowler ploughing engines. Last rites of a different kind.

The end of our tribute to the SMJ. Broom station, where it linked with the Midland Railway's Ashchurch to Redditch line.

SMJ *Beware of Trains* sign – now in my little collection.

industrial building before that, you can't get much sense of the busy railway that once was such a key part of the town. Nowadays, part of the old embankment is still there and also a bridge just east of Towcester station.

I cannot imagine that it is possible to do these walks today, as there would be little to see except endless undergrowth. But for Bryan and for me, the SMJ lives on in the memories of those walks fifty years ago and the priceless photographs we have in our collections.

'May I Remove That Sign?'

A few months ago I saw a cast iron SMJ 'Beware of the Trains' sign for sale at an auction and I was delighted to acquire it. Back in 1966, when the SMJ was being dismantled, we heard that one person had gone along the line and removed all the remaining signs of this type. I'm not sure whether this is true, but, certainly when I set out to find one around this time, they had all gone. I do have a cast iron SMJ weight restriction notice. In those days I was a young trainee reporter on the *Northampton Chronicle and Echo* newspaper and keen not to get into trouble of any kind. I had seen a sign on a bridge near Roade and actually asked the station manager at Northampton Castle if I could take it. How times have changed – imagine doing this today! He kindly agreed and it has been in my very small collection of relics for fifty years. Bryan has one too, but he also has a signal box sign from Ravenstone Wood. His father loaned us his nice Bedford van, ideal for those Sunday afternoon jaunts which might procure, for example, a relic from the undergrowth. I might also add that for most of those walks, I lugged along a battery-operated portable tape recorder, into which I made comments on what we saw. It was from these I typed up my notes and I still have the tapes, tiny reel-to-reel affairs that have not been played for fifty years.

SMJ weight restriction notice in July 1965 near Stoke Bruerne. 'May I please remove that sign?' I asked.

MOTOR CAR ACTS, 1896 AND 1903.
NOTICE.
THIS BRIDGE IS INSUFFICIENT TO CARRY A HEAVY MOTOR CAR THE REGISTERED AXLE WEIGHT OF ANY AXLE OF WHICH EXCEEDS THREE TONS, OR THE REGISTERED AXLE WEIGHTS OF THE SEVERAL AXLES OF WHICH EXCEED IN THE AGGREGATE FIVE TONS, OR A HEAVY MOTOR CAR DRAWING A TRAILER IF THE REGISTERED AXLE WEIGHTS OF THE SEVERAL AXLES OF THE HEAVY MOTOR CAR AND THE AXLE WEIGHTS OF THE SEVERAL AXLES OF THE TRAILER EXCEED IN THE AGGREGATE FIVE TONS.
STRATFORD-UPON-AVON AND MIDLAND JUNCTION RAILWAY.

The same sign, which I have now owned for fifty years – longer than the SMJ existed.

The SMJ is just a memory, but it still manages to intrigue railway historians. Several excellent books and magazine articles have been published about it over the years, Arthur Jordan's wonderful social history being especially good. And J. M. Dunn's little Oakwood Press books are an excellent introduction – my tatty 1953 edition introduced me to the line way back in my youth.

You can learn a lot by paying your last respects to a railway in this way – by walking the line and experiencing it first-hand. In the case of the SMJ, it was all too easy to see why it spent its life flirting with financial failure. It was more than just a rural railway; it was positively pastoral. The setting always dominated the railway, but that environment clearly provided little local traffic potential, either for freight or passenger trains. It seems astonishing that as late as the 1950s pick-up goods trains pottered along the line doing business at the tiny stations. We also came to understand its character and the ambitious pride in building vast stations at Stoke Bruerne and Salcey Forest, which generated almost nothing in the way of passenger traffic. On the rest of the route dainty, much more modest stations sufficed.

You also get to understand that the main features of the line are not always the ones you expect. If I look back at the SMJ, my impressions are of some fairly steep gradients, twin-arch bridges that provided capacity for double tracks that were never needed and small stations with a charm that far outweighed the lowly stature of the line's main station at Stratford-upon-Avon. I think we also shared that walking experience with those engineers back in the 1860s and 1870s who envisaged the route of the line and the promoters who must have stood at various points there many times, determined that it would eventually be built. It totalled 76 miles (including some running powers) but today only the short distance between Fenny Compton station and Kineton Ministry of Defence depot, maybe a mile or two, still exists.

I advise not walking it.

The Great Central

Far too much has been written about the Great Central's untimely demise to warrant yet another account of how the London Midland Region became unwilling adoptive parents and sent their new acquisition off to slaughter. If you lived near the line, you could almost imagine it didn't exist. The Great Central tucked itself away in vast, shallow cuttings, occasionally springing to visual life across magnificent viaducts, or swinging through island platforms at distinctively designed stations. It was all good for the enthusiast. Even as late as 1963, just three years before closure, a few hours at Leicester Central station could be very rewarding. On a sunny summer Saturday, a stream of trains passed through; on such days even the odd V2 might make an appearance, but by then London Midland types dominated. On one occasion I remember seeing all three London Midland Class 7P 4-6-0 – a rebuilt Jubilee, a rebuilt Patriot and a couple of Royal Scots – within a few hours. You might also see a Great Western Grange or Hall with an inter-regional express. Not too many Eastern Region types would be present, but certainly the odd B1 4-6-0 was a welcome sight.

This is the evening train from Nottingham to Rugby on the Great Central Railway headed by Class 5 4-6-0 No. 44872. We travelled from Nottingham to Rugby Central. Here we see the train at Leicester Central on 5 August 1965.

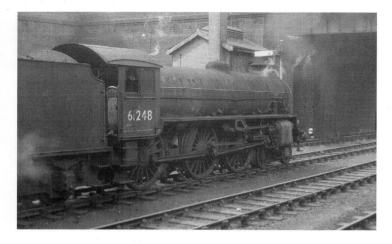

Class B1 No. 61248 *Geoffrey Gibbs* rumbles through the cathedral-like atmosphere of Nottingham Victoria station on 5 August 1965.

The evening stopper from Nottingham to Rugby headed by Class 5 No. 44872. The train is here standing at East Leake station on 5 August 1965.

At Nottingham Victoria station on 6 August 1965, B1 No. 61188 has just coupled up to some parcels vans. It was a pretty busy day at the station, which we reached on the morning train from Rugby Central. I assume she is acting as station pilot.

Of course, right up to 1965 there were the freights, fast-moving, usually headed by a stud of well-maintained Class 9F 2-10-0s from Annesley shed and worked more intensively than those on the neighbouring Midland and East Coast Main Lines, which had a distinctly lackadaisical air to their progress. To watch a Great Central 9F hurry past was an event. With flailing coupling rods, a grimy but effective locomotive would race past, hauling a long train of mineral wagons that clattered across the countryside. They hardly seemed to slow down for stations. The well-engineered Great Central route meant these freights blasted past the island platforms like a sudden stormy shower, with the smell of coal smoke and the last clack of the brake van hitting the rail joints left to impress the watchers. We knew the stretch of the line from Nottingham Victoria to Woodford Halse best. In many ways, this was the essence of the Great Central, the famous and modestly titled 'London Extension' built just before the turn of the century.

Nottingham Victoria was a fairly common destination for us, especially on our 'Runabout Week.' These Runabout tickets gave seven days unlimited travel in much of the East Midlands, so one way to start the day was to catch a local service from Northampton to Rugby Midland, walk the mile or so to Rugby Central and then catch a train to Nottingham Victoria. Highlighting the insularity of the route, we then needed to hop on a trolley bus to reach Nottingham Midland, and return to the rail network proper. The cost of the runabout ticket was *7s 6d* (38p). Not bad for a week's travel and you can be sure we used it for all seven days and always got home late.

A down 'runner' awakens sleepy Nottingham Victoria station on 4 August 1965. In charge is Class WD 2-8-0 No. 90337.

Above: Looking north at Nottingham Victoria station on 4 August 1965. This is platform 10 and a train is about to pass through its majestic setting.

Left: It all looks very quiet at Nottingham Victoria on 4 August 1965, but there were passenger trains still running and regular freights. Thirteen months later through services were withdrawn, with full closure following shortly after.

Above: Last rites at Nottingham Victoria station. It's only a few months since the last train ran, but already the station is reduced to a shell on 3 February 1968. (Bryan Jeyes)

Right: The wonderful craftsmanship that was such a feature of Nottingham Victoria station was no deterrent to the demolition men. Seen here in 1967 with a year to go before demolition. (Bryan Jeyes)

A crane stands in the forecourt at Nottingham Victoria on 3 February 1968 and piles of rubble and scrap litter the scene. (Bryan Jeyes)

I liked those journeys on the Great Central best. At that time the M1 was being built north of Rugby. I don't think we had any clue that the Great Central would not last the decade as we headed north east, sometimes returning along the Great Central again at the end of the day.

When it became clear in 1966 that this vast undertaking truly was going to disappear, I was keen to travel over the whole line. Of course, this was not easy by normal trains, as the line had been basically chopped up into three sections. There was the stretch from London Marylebone to Nottingham, with its intermittent and threatened passenger service; the route north of Nottingham to Sheffield, which had already lost its local passenger trains; and the Woodhead route from Sheffield to Manchester – still busy with both passengers and freight, but being run down. The trick was in trying to travel over the whole route. We had already done the Rugby to Nottingham section regularly, so Bryan and I made plans to catch a train from Rugby Central to Marylebone. Having started work, our financial constraints imposed by pocket money had disappeared. So we travelled to Rugby Midland one very misty morning in the spring of 1966 and trod the well-worn path to Rugby Central station.

There is a delicious naivety to youth. When we first went to Rugby in the late 1950s it was to see trains on the West Coast Main Line. It so happened that the field in which we were camped had a great view of the traffic entering Rugby shed, trains setting off to Market Harborough and Peterborough and also the series of bridges and viaducts that carried the GCR through Rugby. It was like a segregated child, aloof from its surroundings and preferring to keep its distance. Surely a link with the other lines at Rugby would have been useful? The first train I ever saw on the Great Central was a southbound freight

Black 5 No. 45222 arrives at an almost deserted Rugby Central station in the mist on 7 April 1966. The Great Central has only five months to live as a through route.

hauled by a North Eastern B16 Class 4-6-0. When the next train was a northbound local passenger service with an L1 Class 2-6-4 tank up front I knew I had stumbled across something special. These types were completely unknown to me, yet here they were, only a 20-minute train ride away. At last I had something to underline in that vast untouched series of pages in my Ian Allan *ABC*. Up until then the only Eastern Region engine I had seen was B1 4-6-0, No. 61001 *Eland*, leaving Northampton for Peterborough. The rest of the day – and several to follow – added endless 9Fs, V-2s and other delights and by 1962 a visit to Rugby was really something to look forward to.

Sadly, it wasn't to last. Here we were just four years later standing on the platform at Rugby Central station. The freights had all gone, diverted to rival lines. The rich variety of steam power had gone as well. Stanier Class 5s hauled virtually everything, and a fairly shoddy bunch they were too. Even the through trains, such as the Bournemouth–York, had been handed over to a bunch of uninteresting Type 3 English Electric diesels.

The contrast between Rugby's two stations was worth contemplating. We had just alighted from a new AM10 electric multiple unit at Rugby Midland's huge northbound platform. You entered the station under a decorative awning and then walked up a long subway passage, arriving in the middle of the platforms. The centrepiece of the station was a vast two-storey building housing endless offices, waiting rooms and other services. Two very long main platforms, north and southbound, were each capable of accommodating two trains. There were also long bays at either end. Lastly, a huge overall roof, covered in soot, stretched out over the running lines with a line of supports between the tracks. It wasn't very beautiful, but it was certainly impressive.

All day long there seemed to be something passing through Rugby Midland, either stopping at the platforms, waiting for a road, or passing through cautiously because of the speed restrictions. To the north of the station were massive yards, junctions to Birmingham, Leamington and Leicester. To the south there was a branch to Market Harborough, a flyover for the Northampton line and a cluster of tall radio masts at Hillmorton. There was also the well-known Rugby Testing Station, built to operate steam locomotives on rollers to collect data. Lastly, there was a big running shed complete with workshops where quite heavy repairs could be carried out. More than one hundred engines were based at Rugby in the 1950s.

Compare this with the more modest Great Central. In fact, if you were standing at the south end of Rugby Midland station, you could see the Great Central's two tracks sweeping imperiously over the West Coast Main Line on a sturdy grey girder bridge, then passing the Testing Station on a long embankment. It seems amazing that all this has gone.

The Great Central's station building was a modest affair with three tiny gables facing the east side of Hillmorton Road. You could drive past it quite easily without noticing it. From here you passed through an ugly glazed passage and descended some stairs to find an island platform of modest proportions – just wide enough to do its job and no more. There were two tracks passing the platforms and two sidings, with a goods yard and goods shed north of the line.

Physically, it was a knockout punch by the London & North Western Railway's impressive edifice. But stand back for a moment, because here comes the Down 'Royal Scot' express passing non-stop through Rugby Midland with fourteen coaches hauled by a green Duchess Class Pacific. It moves steadily but cautiously through the station, an athlete awaiting orders to go. It's quite humiliating to watch such an impressive service reduced to making such tedious progress, but such is the 45 mph speed limit through the station that every express train's progress is impeded in this way. The speedy Great Central must have allowed itself a smug grin.

To Marylebone and Back

Now we are at Rugby Central. A train is signalled from the north and here it comes, making very good speed. The train races by, yet it's a freight comprising a long line of rattling mineral wagons with a 9F 2-10-0 freight engine up front. We can't visualise an express racing through because, unlike at Rugby Midland, the major named trains (*The Master Cutler* and *The South Yorkshireman*) both stop at Rugby Central.

So here we are, on 7 April 1966, with those two named trains just a memory and the only remaining passenger services what are delightfully called 'semi-fasts.' These trains are not really fast at all and since our motive power is likely to be a clapped-out Stanier Class 5, we are not expecting great things. Soon a train appears through the mist from the north. It's a local service terminating at Rugby and the coaches are quickly reversed into the Down siding. Shortly after, the 09.30 to Marylebone is signalled and as the mist starts to evaporate, it turns up headed by an old friend.

The 09.30 to Marylebone arrives at Rugby Central on 7 April 1966, behind No. 45190. She's come down in the world since I photographed her looking pristine a year earlier, but the train is still a Class 1 job.

Here is No. 45190, whose footplate we shared on that last day at Northampton shed. Well, we are in for a good run after all. With safety valves healthily blowing off, and a handful of passengers loaded aboard, we set off from Rugby. Our Black 5 seems to still be in good nick, although I don't think she's been cleaned since we last saw her at Northampton six months earlier. The two oil lamps over the buffers flicker with an orange glow. We have an express headcode and the driver roars impressively away through the long cutting that takes the Great Central towards the open Warwickshire countryside. Our first stop is Woodford Halse and it's with sadness that we look across to the huge array of abandoned sidings and the once important motive power depot, all now bereft of life. We think of places like Swindon and Derby as railway towns; well, in its own way, so was Woodford Halse. A village of a few hundred people rapidly expanded with the coming of the railway until it housed around 2,000 inhabitants, with the railway dominating every facet of its life. In my capacity as a newspaper reporter, I gathered a group of former railwaymen together just after the Great Central closed in September 1966 to talk about the way their lives and that of Woodford itself, would change. I think this was at a staff club of some kind – I recall a large and impressive banner representing the railway trades unions. Sadly this article is not in my file of cuttings from my *Northampton Chronicle and Echo* days. However, I clearly recall the bitter look on their faces.

Our next stop is Brackley Central. By the lineside stands a tall water tower, but the adjacent goods shed is already devoid of tracks, following the withdrawal of freight services. The Class 5's whistle hoots across the valley and our train heads off across yet another huge viaduct. Not too long after the Great Central closed, this impressive structure was demolished. Drive along the A43 past Brackley today and you'll find it hard to see any trace of the railway, although the station building clings to life in use as a tyre company workshop.

From Brackley to Aylesbury, the Great Central ran through miles of unspoilt countryside. In fact the whole of our journey from Rugby to Aylesbury, which takes about an hour, seems to scrupulously avoid any towns or villages that could be important (apart from Brackley, perhaps). Aylesbury still has some bustle about it when we arrive. With a regular diesel multiple unit service to Marylebone, Aylesbury marks the point where we return to civilisation. After a brief pause we are off again, and soon our train runs alongside the Underground services through Harrow-on-the-Hill and into Marylebone. Of all London's terminus stations, this was probably the least attractive in the 1960s. For a start it is too quiet, the stillness being punctuated by the odd train arriving. A glance around indicates that not too many passengers are on our mid-morning arrival from Rugby.

We travel home on the 16.30 from Marylebone. A very grubby Class 5, No. 44825, but with clean cab sides, hauls the train. It clearly is not in the best condition, as her crew are off at every station carefully examining the motion. We eventually arrive back at Rugby Central after a rather sad, but fascinating day out. And at least we have achieved one objective – with our previous trips between Rugby and Nottingham we have now travelled on all the southern section of the Great Central by train. Now, how about the section from Nottingham northwards?

Part of it we never did. But the rest, from Colwick to Manchester, was conveniently advertised as being covered by a rail tour on 26 March 1966, which somehow wove

Having brought in the morning Nottingham–London service, which we caught at Rugby Central, No. 45190 is seen here backing out of Marylebone station on 7 April 1966. This was a month spent doing lots of photography, too much of it in the rain.

Cowlick Black 5 No. 44825 stands at Marylebone with the 16.38 to Nottingham on 7 April 1966. Although it kept time, I noticed the driver was out at every station inspecting the motion. The GC was in its dying days.

We have now reached Rugby Central station on our journey from London Marylebone on 7 April 1966. The Class 5 is getting another quick check over from the driver. The rust-streaked engine has been given a bit of dignity as someone has cleaned the cabside. This was the engine that sadly failed on 3 September 1966, the last day of GC services, having been specially cleaned by Colwick shed. GC drivers always preferred B1s and Standard Class 5s.

its way from Leicester Midland station to Colwick on the Great Central. Here a B1 4-6-0 hauled us to a point just north of Sheffield Victoria, where the pioneer Class EM1 electric engine, No. 26000 *Tommy*, took over for the run through the Woodhead Tunnel. Sadly passengers were not able to get off at any point while *Tommy* was hauling the train, so I have no photographs.

A few months later, on 3 September 1966, I managed to persuade the Chief Reporter that it was worthwhile my reporting the end of the Great Central. I drove over to Brackley on what was a gloomy late afternoon and joined the throng of people at Central station to watch a Merchant Navy Class 4-6-2, No. 35030 *Elder Dempster Lines*, rush through heading south with The Great Central Rail Tour. It seemed somehow completely inappropriate; surely the last train should have been hauled by one of the Eastern Region engines which gave the Great Central its pride? A couple of B1s double headed would have done nicely.

On 12 November 1966, Leicester Central (a spacious, main line station) had been reduced to an unstaffed halt for local trains between Rugby Central and Nottingham following closure of the Great Central as a through route. This sad view shows signal arms missing and no one in sight. It's hard to imagine an A3 halting here with the Up 'Master Cutler' for Marylebone. The years 1964–66 saw our railway system ravaged. (Bryan Jeyes)

Woodford Halse: The Demise of a Steam Railway Town

In January 1967, Bryan and I decided to take a last look at Woodford Halse station. He managed to borrow his father's 1964 Bedford Utilabrake (a van with windows and, in the back, slatted wooden seats) and drove carefully on a snowy Sunday through the Northamptonshire countryside to Woodford Halse. The Great Central's southern extension had been closed for four months, so this would be something of a pilgrimage.

The entrance to Woodford Halse station was highly inauspicious. You walked through a door beneath an overbridge that had a postbox built into the wall and set of steps heading upwards. The gates were not locked so we parked the Bedford and walked up the stairs and onto the platforms. The sky was heavy with low clouds, ready to deposit further snow on the dismal surroundings. Everywhere there was silence, as though the snow had damped out any sound. Our feet crunched on the white carpet as we moved along the deserted platforms. Somewhere a distant church clock rang out the hour. We started off by walking to the north end. Even though some rails had been removed, there was still a mass of track work sweeping round a bend to the right and past the vast, but now silent, area which so recently had been hectic marshalling yards and a busy engine shed. It was so strange, as there was absolutely no one about. I felt as though at seven o'clock tomorrow the place would be bursting with life, with passengers getting warm in the waiting room while station staff were busy with parcels and greeting a non-stop flow of trains. We stood on the footbridge and took photographs, imagining the *Master Cutler* rushing through on its way to Sheffield behind a V2 2-6-2, followed by a local from Banbury arriving with a Thompson L1 tank up front.

Back to reality. To the south was a sturdy water column and a signal box at the junction of the spur to the Stratford-upon-Avon & Midland Junction line to Byfield and the west. A double bracket starter signal, devoid of its arms, stood watch over the end of the platform. The only track that seemed to have gone was a long siding on the east side of the line. In the distance was a solid three-arch bridge, but the blanket of snow seemed to have lent an especially gloomy air to the distant view.

Ever one to explore, Bryan was soon poking around in the undergrowth at the base of some telegraph poles. Well, well, well – now we knew where the signal arms had gone. They had just been thrown into a weedy patch by the side of the line that had once been the site of a triple arm signal ... and covered in snow. It was the work of a few minutes to load one aboard the Bedford van – that's what they were built for. After half an hour we left the station, slid the Bedford's doors shut and gunned its heater. The sky was dark when we arrived home.

It wasn't long before the rails were removed and Woodford Halse, railway town for sixty-seven years, found itself looking for a new existence. I flew over the site a few years ago in a light aircraft and it's amazing how rapidly nature works to obliterate any trace of a railway. True, you could see the route of the tracks by the lines of recently grown hedges, but yards and stations and most bridges seemed to have completely disappeared. Take a look at Google Earth and you'll see what I mean.

Farewell Great Central. It was good to have known you.

The view from Woodford Halse on the January day mentioned in the text. Here we are looking north from the footbridge with the huge yards on the right.

Now looking south at Woodford Halse, we see water cranes, signals with no arms and a bridge in the distance that still stands.

Crewe's Steam Finale

While some enthusiasts couldn't get enough of steam's final hours, I felt an overwhelming sense of depression when considering the demise of such an old friend. I was fortunate to reside in Britain at the time; in California, where I lived for quite a few years, friends of my age had never seen steam locomotives in normal service. (They also have very few heritage steam trains and find it amazing that dozens of steam engines are regularly at work in the UK). The last time I went to see steam on my favourite region, the London Midland, was in February 1967. I remember that day – the papers were full of the news that Donald Campbell had lost his life trying to break the water speed record in his boat *Bluebird*. We planned to make two shed visits – to Crewe South and Chester. Crewe North had already closed, so from the station, where a couple of Stanier Black 5s were at work, we headed for Crewe South. My photos from that day show not a single clean engine at work.

This was to be the last year when you could see a Britannia Pacific in normal service (with the exception of *Oliver Cromwell*). Two of my favourite Britannias were on shed, Nos 70046 *Anzac* and 70047. Both were very dirty and both had the high-sided tender fitted to the later members of the class. They had also been long-term Midland Region engines, rather than part of the mammoth cascading of these locomotives to the West Coast Main Line when the Eastern and Western Regions could find no further work for them. I recall seeing No. 70005 *John Milton* one evening in March 1963 heading a southbound freight near Roade station and could hardly believe it. The last time I had seen this engine it had been in East Anglia. To prove this was no freak, No. 70000 *Britannia* turned up at Northampton station carrying a Willesden (1A) shed plate a few days later on a local from Euston. Only when *Trains Illustrated* appeared did we realise that the hoard of Britannias at March depot had been shifted to the London Midland Region. This shouldn't have been too much of a surprise. We had visited March in 1962 and found no fewer than eleven of them inside the shed on a Saturday morning, most of them appearing to be in store. While this was great for our spotting books – all of a sudden I only needed one Britannia, No. 70037 *Hereward the Wake*, to clear them – it heralded a mass onslaught of our London Midland Class 7P engines. Some of these, examples in poor condition, were transferred to the Great Central to give nightmares to the good folk at Annesley depot. Others were withdrawn and by the summer of 1964 a Royal Scot, rebuilt Patriot or rebuilt Jubilee was a rare sight south of Crewe.

At Crewe South, Nos 70046 and 70047 were joined by an Eastern Region refugee – No. 70038 *Robin Hood*. As we wandered round the vast shed, still busy and with no diesels present, it was easy to see why steam had had its day. A group of fitters were busy doing a piston examination on a Class 5 in the open – on a biting cold February morning. The ground was covered with soot and ash, smoke swirled around the air and the only clean locomotive was 2-6-0 No. 78036 – and that was withdrawn! These were the working conditions of a bygone age. It was a salutary thought that not one engine we saw at Crewe South would exist eighteen months later, save for Southern region electric engine No. E5003, which was awaiting conversion to an electro-diesel. Ten years later, this one also felt the cutter's torch.

After watching some trains pass the complex junctions north of Crewe, we headed for Chester's magnificent station and stood outside for a few minutes admiring the architecture. Then it was off to the shed. It seems remarkable that only eighteen months from the end of steam, we were visiting two engine sheds with not a single diesel in sight.

Crewe South was quite a neat and tidy depot, even on 13 February 1967 when its role was coming to an end. It still had dozens of engines on shed, many having worked in from Carlisle. Typical of these is Britannia No. 70038 *Robin Hood*, seen here in unlined green livery. She was withdrawn in August 1967.

Two engines brewing up ready to leave Crewe South (5B) on 13 February 1967 are Class 8F 2-8-0 No. 48449 and Britannia No. 70046 *Anzac*. These were the times when today's majestic workhorse was tomorrow's 100 tons of scrap. *Anzac* was a favourite from the Holyhead expresses, now in straitened circumstances and with only four months to live.

A picture which epitomises the confusing end of steam. Steam, diesel and electric are together at Crewe on 21 May 1964. The Royal Scot, No. 46155 *The Lancer* is preparing to head a northbound express. Class 40 No. D304 is on the left and an early AC electric waits for a Manchester service.

Here we see Jinty No. 47410 on its way from Holyhead (6J), where it was withdrawn in September 1966, to George Cohen's yard at Cransley, Kettering, Northants for scrapping. This took place in April 1967. Meanwhile, the rather decrepit looking engine is having a pause at Chester shed on 13 February 1967 with a withdrawn Standard Class 4 2-6-0 alongside. Notice the ominous tag on the Jinty's vertical handrail, detailing where the engine was to be sent for breaking up. This locomotive gave forty years of service. Something is fixed to the top lamp bracket, but I can't work out what.

Like Crewe South, Chester seemed to have an open invitation to railway enthusiasts. People just got on with their jobs as we wandered around, taking care when walking over rails. These were the last days of steam on the Birkenhead to Paddington through trains and the engine that had hauled that day's morning service as far as Chester, a Stanier 2-6-4T, was cooling off after its exertions. The depot was full of BR Standard and ex-LMS types, some of them in store having finished their working career. One locomotive present was a Jinty 0-6-0T with a tag on its handrail indicating that it was in transit from its home at Holyhead to George Cohen at Kettering, our own local breaker's yard. Also standing looking very sorry for itself was the very first Class 5 4-6-0 to be ordered (but actually not the first to be built) No. 45000. I was surprised to hear later that it was resuscitated and put back to work. This engine was already on the list of locomotives designated for preservation. It was taken out of service later in 1967 and eventually restored to service. I saw it a few months ago in the National Railway Museum at Shildon looking resplendent in LMS black.

Another Jinty tank, No. 47673 – this one from Llandudno Junction shed. Like the others she was in (very protracted) transit to a scrapyard. She was one of the last to be built – at Horwich in 1931. Although withdrawn in November 1966, she was still at Chester in June 1967. Last rites sometimes took time.

A decent paint job is no barrier to the call of the scrap man. Here we see a nice clean Standard Class 2, No. 78036, but the lack of a front number plate and the missing connecting rod tell the real story. Crewe South scrap line, 13 February 1967.

That was it for London Midland steam. After I walked out of Chester shed, I never saw another LMS engine at work in normal service. Yet there is a small postscript. In late June 1968, a few weeks before steam ended, I was sent to Wigan to attend a course run by United Newspapers and saw a few redundant Class 5 and Class 8F steam locomotives covered in filth and rust at various points by the lineside. I prefer to remember that day at Crewe and Chester as my last look at Midland steam.

Racing to the Seaside

Family holidays in the 1950s and 1960s were always at the seaside. Unfortunately for me, our dad hired – and later bought – a car for these trips, so any chance of train travel was ruled out. However, in the early 1960s we started going to Bournemouth each year, so things were looking up. The first year I found that Bournemouth West station was only a ten minute walk from our hotel, so I wandered off there as often as I could without wishing to leave my brother Nick on his own too much. My first visit was on a Sunday and standing at the end of the platform was West Country Class 4-6-2 No. 34038 *Lynton*. I showed some interest in the engine to the crew and straightaway was invited on to the footplate, being treated to a demonstration of the radical pedal-operated firehole doors. I could get to like living on the Southern Region.

A few years later, Bryan and I were chatting about paying our last respects to Southern steam. It hardly seemed possible that it was all about to end, only a few years after that day at Bournemouth. But so much water had swirled under the bridge over the past six years. At the end of 1962, the stroke of an accountant's pen saw off a number of Southern types including all the neat little K Class 2-6-0s. The Lord Nelson, Schools and King Arthur classes were also rendered extinct. The first original Bulleid Pacifics went in 1963 and in 1964 the first rebuilds and Merchant Navy engines hit the scrapheap. Yet there was plenty still to admire. It seemed odd that a railway which focused most of its efforts on electrification ended up having the last all-steam main line in the country.

How should we celebrate the last rites of Southern steam? This was a main line and we wanted to see trains travelling fast. In the end we decided that we would visit a new venue where we could see steam passing at express speed, so Hook in Hampshire was selected. Happily, 4 March 1967 turned out to be a very sunny day – ideal weather for photography. Hook had two widely spaced platforms with four tracks, and what was clearly once an island platform between the two. This had obviously not been used for years, as it was covered in grass with a signal box at the north end. We decided to position ourselves on the Down platform with the sun behind us.

It was such a pleasant experience. The sun kept shining all day – not bad for March – and the trains just kept on coming. An old friend, No. 35008 *Orient Line*, was first to appear, rather dirty but still carrying its nameplates. There followed a succession of interesting trains, all hauled by Bulleid Pacifics except one with a blue Warship diesel and a test train with an electro-diesel up front.

Standing apart from the other engines at Eastleigh on 6 December 1964 was a withdrawn Stanier Class 5 and this Battle of Britain class Pacific, No. 34067 *Tangmere*. She had been withdrawn more than a year earlier, in November 1963, but was still awaiting the call to the scrapyard. The crests have been crudely removed by oxy-acetylene cutter and she lacks the middle tender wheels. Happily she was later rescued from the breaker's yard and is currently working back on the main line.

All is not what it seems. No. 35001 *Channel Packet*, the first of the Merchant Navy Pacifics, looks all ready to work the next day. She's nicely clean and has a headcode disc on the front. Yet this engine had been withdrawn two weeks earlier and was actually awaiting removal for scrap. Unlike nearly all the other withdrawn engines at Eastleigh this day, No. 35001 did not go to Barry scrapyard, which would have provided an escape route into preservation for this significant engine. Picture taken on 6 December 1964.

Her working life apparently over, Battle of Britain class Pacific No. 34072 *257 Squadron* awaits her fate at Eastleigh on 6 December 1964. She is still nice and clean, having been withdrawn from Eastleigh shed two months before I took this picture. No. 34072 survived her whole life with a high-sided tender. After a spell at Barry scrapyard, she was eventually returned to steam by the experts at Southern Locomotives Ltd.

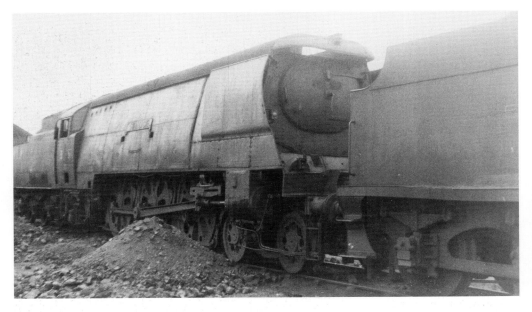

Another reasonably clean Bullied Pacific is about to head for the scrapyard. This is No. 34105 *Swanage*, an engine I knew well having been hauled by it on the Pines Express. Oblivion seemed to be her destiny, but eventually she was rescued for further service. She is seen here at Eastleigh on 6 December 1964.

I also recall seeing No. 35030 *Elder Dempster Lines* heading for Waterloo, very grimy but still carrying nameplates and going like the wind with a very youthful fireman on board. Then came the icing on the cake, as a spotless original West Country came past, No. 34102 *Lapford*, one of a handful of unrebuilt engines remaining in service. It seemed like a very appropriate valedictory trip and my photographs were excellent. Not a bad way to pay homage to express steam in the UK.

The end of Southern steam – Merchant Navy Pacific No. 35008 *Orient Line* races through Hook on 4 March 1967, with Southern steam in its dying days. She has lost her front number plate but still carries her nameplates.

Class 4 4-6-0 No. 75077, in filthy condition, is passing through Hook on 4 March 1967. She is one of those fitted with a double chimney and high-sided tender and is running light engine with a West Country Pacific. Four months later she was withdrawn for scrap.

On 4 March 1967 we see No. 35030 *Elder Dempster Lines* racing through Hook station with an express for London. She still carries nameplates at this late stage in her career, but a clean would have been nice.

Salvation for one Bulleid Pacific No. 34016 *Bodmin* – after being rescued from Barry scrapyard, this West Country went first of all to Quainton Road, where it is seen on 29 April 1973. Later it was moved to the Mid Hants Railway for full restoration. It seemed a miracle at the time that someone would try to restore such a big engine.

From 20,000 to Three

When British Railways was created in 1948, the four private railway companies handed over about 20,000 steam locomotives and one main line diesel. That was the LMS locomotive No. 10000, shortly to be joined by its sister, No. 10001. The Great Western Railway had ordered a pair of gas turbine engines for evaluation; the Southern had diesel locomotives on order and electrics Nos CC1 and CC2 in service, and the LNER's electrification of the Woodhead route was only delayed by the intervention of the Second World War. How different things might have been had the LMS continued to exist as, if trials with the two new diesels had proved successful, the company had plans to invest heavily in modern traction. In the end they did prove successful, after some teething troubles, and became a regular sight paired together on the Royal Scot service from Euston to Glasgow.

Yet those 20,000 steam locomotives ruled the day and construction of types already ordered by the four private companies continued apace while Robert Riddles and his (mainly ex-LMS) team got down to designing the new BR Standard classes. In fact the Railway Correspondence and Travel Society has compiled a table showing that more than 1500 of the pre-1948 types were built, including dozens of obsolete 9400 class Western Region pannier tanks, still in production as late as 1956. As if to force home the point, withdrawals of the 9400 class started only three years after the last new one was delivered.

Swindon scrapyard. A very long time after she was withdrawn (back in April 1961), this little 0-4-2T, No. 5815, clung to life. Here she is in company with railcar No. W21W and Hall 4-6-0 No. 5904 *Kelham Hall* on 10 May 1964. No. 5815 was the last survivor of the 5800s and was formerly based at Swindon shed, who used it on local freights. I have no idea why she was still around three years after withdrawal. In the end, both these engines were cut up in South Wales.

Patricroft shed near Manchester at the very end, with a rusty Standard Class 5 and an 8F awaiting removal for scrap, captured from a very unusual angle. (Bob Mullins)

The Modernisation Plan, which spelled the end of steam traction, led to widespread orders for untried diesel locomotives – sometimes just ten of one type, but other classes were ordered in large quantities. Writing in 1959, historian Henry Casserley said that when the Modernisation Plan was completed, there would be 7,000 steam engines still at work. With Bullied Pacifics still being rebuilt as late as 1961, it was widely accepted that these types, at least, would have a useful role to play well into the 1970s. The same was true of the Class 9F 2-10-0s, which were seen as having a viable long-term future. After all, who would build a big fleet of excellent new freight engines and scrap them within a third of their economic life? I say a third, in fact quite a few of the last built engines, including the preserved trio Nos 92214, 92219 and 92220 *Evening Star*, enjoyed fewer than six years in service.

Two factors meant that a measured approach to eliminating steam was discarded, Firstly, the number of lines and services, both passenger and freight, being closed accelerated the demise of the steam locomotive. Diesel multiple units appeared on many lines which then lost their passenger services, allowing them to be cascaded elsewhere to eliminate steam. The mindset of BR also changed. Partly driven by the difficulty of recruiting people to tackle dirty and unhygienic work, and partly for ideological and image reasons, BR decided to press ahead with their rather ramshackle fleet of modern traction and force the demise of the steam locomotive.

By 1962, Casserley's 7,000 figure was under threat. In the middle of the year the following steam locomotives were at work:

Western Region	1,913 locomotives of 32 classes
Southern Region	617 locomotives of 27 classes
London Midland Region	4,211 locomotives of 45 classes
Eastern Region	1,992 locomotives of 39 classes
BR Standard	999 locomotives of 12 classes
Ex-WD	739 locomotives of 2 classes
Total	10,471 locomotives of 157 classes

Of those 157 classes, thirty comprised fewer than ten locomotives and were shortly to be eliminated.

In fact, 1962 was a seismic year in the efforts to reduce the steam locomotive fleet. It saw the end of a number of famous types, such as the Great Western King class, the Midland Princess and unrebuilt Patriot, the Southern Schools, Lord Nelsons and King Arthurs and Eastern N2, N7, L1 and K3s. It was also the year when a start was made on scrapping many stalwart types such as the Duchess, A4 and A1 Pacifics and the first BR Standard types. In short, from 1962 onwards, every steam engine was vulnerable. By the end of the year, East Anglia was virtually steam free and the south east of Britain was heading that way.

Two years later, in the middle of 1964, a startling change had taken place. Locomotives in service comprised:

Western Region	946 locomotives of 27 classes
Southern Region	224 locomotives of 10 classes
London Midland Region	2,712 locomotives of 26 classes
Eastern Region	680 locomotives of 17 classes
BR Standard	949 locomotives of 11 classes
Ex-WD	461 locomotives of 1 class
Total	5,511 locomotives of 92 classes

This is the scrap line at Crewe South on February 13 1967 – only four engines present. Leading them is Class 5 4-6-0 No. 45033, a very early Vulcan Foundry engine with domeless boiler. With the connecting rod tied to the running plate, she's all ready for her last journey. She was the fourteenth Class 5 to be built.

Cransley scrapyard, near Kettering on a pleasant spring day – 5 March 1967. A batch of engines from the Birmingham area has arrived for breaking and here is Class 8F 2-8-0 No. 48755 with a shed code that indicates she has arrived from 2E – Saltley. The engine still has its connecting rods in place. Usually these were removed before movement to a scrapyard.

At Canklow depot near Sheffield on 5 August 1965 is Ivatt 2-6-0 No. 43064 with B1 No. 61190. We see typical South Yorkshire scenery and an old Great Northern Railway tender standing behind the 2-6-0. Notice the wagons on the coaling stage. The two engines were withdrawn in June 1965 and are about to make the short journey to Ward's scrapyard at Beighton.

Another Ivatt 2-6-0, this time No. 43091, seen at its home depot of Canklow, Sheffield, is awaiting transport for scrap. She will go to Ward's yard at Killamarsh where, two months later, she will exist only as scrap. She looks in quite good order, with a tablet catcher from her days on the old Midland and Great Northern Joint line. 5 August 1965.

On August 5 1965, Canklow depot (41D) was host to a number of B1s. This one, No. 61093, is seen near the water tower on 5 August 1965. She had been withdrawn from Langwith Junction a few days earlier and was on her way to a scrapyard near Rotherham.

The Western Region declared at that time it would be rid of standard gauge steam by the end of 1965; all Great Western engines were withdrawn, plus many BR Standard types. Those in the best condition, including some 9Fs, were transferred to the London Midland Region. These figures also show the drastic reduction in Eastern Region types. Hardly a month went by at this period without the last members of a well-loved class being taken out of service. Only three classes remained intact. These were the Britannias, the Standard Class 4 4-6-0s and the Standard Class 3 2-6-0s. By the middle of November 1965, this was the picture:

Western Region	147 locomotives of 11 classes
Southern Region	113 locomotives of 7 classes
London Midland Region	1,790 locomotives of 20 classes
Eastern Region	330 locomotives of 14 classes
BR Standard	722 locomotives of 11 classes
Ex-WD	255 locomotives of 1 class
Total	3,357 locomotives of 64 classes

A pair of Austerity 2-8-0s and a B1 4-6-0 await the end at Wakefield shed (56A) in the summer of 1967. These engines did years of hard work in Yorkshire. (Bob Mullins)

End of the line for a Stanier 8F at Newton Heath shed (9D) in July 1968. The last day of steam was four weeks away. (Bob Mullins)

Above: This engine, Ivatt 2-6-0 No. 46401, had been withdrawn the previous month and is seen here at Buxton on 30 June 1966 awaiting movement to a scrapyard. The second Ivatt Class 2 to be built, it originally worked out of Kettering on the line to Huntingdon.

Left: Last rites for a one-time Midland and Great Northern line Ivatt Class 4, No. 43147. She's in transit at Northampton shed on her way to Eastleigh and then to Cashmore's at Newport for scrap. She has already been withdrawn and is seen here on 7 March 1965. The connecting rod is tied on the running plate.

Of the totals above, it seems amazing that in November 1965 the Western Region had nearly 150 steam engines on its books; yet by the end of the year they had no standard gauge engines at all. What happened to all the work being done by these engines? In less than three years, the remaining 3,357 steam engines still at work would be withdrawn, an amazing feat, even considering new diesel deliveries. Our last look at the reduction of steam is at the end of 1967:

Western Region	3 locomotives of 1 class (Vale of Rheidol narrow gauge engines)
Southern Region	0 locomotives
London Midland Region	351 locomotives of 3 classes
Eastern Region	1 locomotive of 1 class (a solitary K1 2-6-0)
BR Standard	78 locomotives of 4 classes
Ex-WD	0 locomotives
Total	433 locomotives of 9 classes

Eight months later it was all over. Preserved Britannia Pacific No. 70013 *Oliver Cromwell* went under its own steam to Norfolk to become a museum piece and BR said good riddance to steam, save for the three Vale of Rheidol narrow gauge engines. BR's steam fleet went from twenty thousand to three in just twenty years. As if to emphasise its loyalty to electrics and diesels, British Rail then banned steam altogether, until in August 1971 a more enlightened view prevailed.

Lurking outside Machynlleth shed on 22 August 1966 is BR Standard Class 4 2-6-0 No. 76043. Here her working days are over and she was withdrawn a few weeks later. The painted shed code (2E, Saltley) is an old one – she was based at Machynlleth when I took this picture. I suspect she had not done much work since arriving from Saltley eight weeks earlier. Poor old 76043 – sadly she's a goner.

Rust-streaked Standard Class 5 4-6-0 No. 73143 (with Caprotti valve gear) is seen here at Patricroft shed (9H) in the summer of 1968 awaiting removal for scrap. She was just twelve years old and had been withdrawn in June 1968. (Bob Mullins)

Jinty tanks awaiting the torch at Cransley, Northamptonshire in 1967. (Bryan Jeyes)

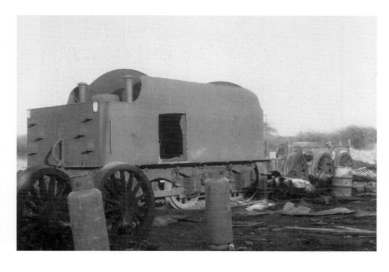

A sad sight at the breaker's yard of George Cohen at Cransley, near Kettering, as a Class 8F 2-8-0 is reduced to scrap. This is 5 March 1967.

On 23 March 1968 *Flying Scotsman* ran from St Pancras to Keighley with a rail tour. She is seen here at Wellingborough, my last picture of steam on BR in the 1960s. She was running early in heavy rain and I hardly had time to get my camera out.

During the summer of 1964, these two withdrawn engines were a familiar sight outside Derby works seen here on 5 August 1964, the front engine is a J94, No. 68013, minus coupling rods. Behind is Jubilee 4-6-0 No. 45585 *Hyderabad*, which had been a Midland line engine since 1937. Both engines would shortly be removed for scrap.

The End of a Steam Era – The Duchess Pacifics

We all have our own memories of those years – provided we are old enough. It is actually a salutary thought that to have reasonable recollections of steam at work on BR you probably need to be in your late fifties now. For our little group of spotters, the ultimate locomotive was always the Duchess. It was less flashy than an A4 or a Merchant Navy and less elaborately decorated than a Great Western King. For us there was nothing to touch it, especially when the London Midland Region started painting them crimson in 1957; we knew that when the Duchesses disappeared, a big chunk of railway enthusiasm would disappear from our lives. The Princess Royal class was almost as good. When I stood on a bridge at Roade station on the West Coast Main Line in the summer of 1960 and watched No. 46200 *The Princess Royal* roar underneath, gleaming in crimson paint, it hardly seemed possible that just over four years later not a single Stanier Pacific would be at work. Bob Mullins, a friend from school, had got me trainspotting again after a couple of years on the sidelines. We usually caught the 08.46 for London out of Northampton on a Saturday and visited a field at Roade right next to the main line. That first summer day in 1960, back with my old Ian Allan spotting books, I was surprised to see Peak No. D3 *Skiddaw* on a northbound express; later D1 *Scafell Pike* was seen heading an Up passenger train. They were a kind of novelty, like 10000 and 10001 had been for many years. Within a year the novelty had worn off for spotters, for the Peaks had been joined by a few of the ungainly English Electric Type 4 engines. Imagine our dismay when in 1962 the prestige Royal Scot service was handed over to these oversized Type 4 engines, which were said to be merely a replacement for Class 7P steam locomotives.

As the new diesels chased away steam power, eventually Camden – the London shed providing top link motive power for the Anglo–Scottish and other principal West Coast expresses – lost its allocation of Duchess Pacifics and then closed. That was in September 1963. The last three Pacifics went to Willesden, where an enthusiastic shed master kept them in spotless condition. *City of Chester*, *City of Coventry* and *City of London* could usually be found on shed on a Saturday morning, our normal time for a visit. One of them was regularly parked outside, possibly with Britannia No. 70020 *Mercury*, which was another of the depot's special 'pets.' Even as late as 1964, on a normal day by the West Coast Main Line, you could expect to see a few Duchess Pacifics. I saw seven during the first week of August 1964, all but one on express passenger work. But trouble was ahead; the Stanier express types, including the Jubilees, Royal Scots and Duchesses, were to be banned from operating under the 25kv electrified wires south of Crewe on 1 September 1964.

Then we heard that the surviving Duchesses were being transferred to the Southern Region. At that time nineteen, or exactly half the class, were still at work. This forced evacuation to the south sounded a real blow, but maybe Waterloo wasn't too far away …

In early September 1964 I went to Crewe works and was delighted to see an old friend in the station – Duchess No. 46240 *City of Coventry* in immaculate condition – coupling up to a northbound express. She was wearing a 5A (Crewe North) shed plate. Little did I realise this would be my last view of a Duchess in normal service. When *Modern Railways* magazine appeared later that month it confirmed an ugly rumour – all the Duchesses except No. 46256 had been withdrawn and the lone survivor had been given a stay of execution just to haul a single final rail tour. This was devastating news. Only one of the final nineteen was saved for preservation, No. 46235 *City of Birmingham*, which was to go on static display in Birmingham Museum of Science and Industry. There was none of the mad clamour that greeted the withdrawal of the A4s, when 60007, 60009 and 60019 were added to the three already set aside for keeps. There was some talk of Lichfield City Council wanting to purchase No. 46250 *City of Lichfield* for display, but nothing came of it. With no real time to organise a campaign to save one, even No. 46256 *Sir William A. Stanier F.R.S.* went to the scrapheap.

The end of the Duchess Pacifics – No. 46235 *City of Birmingham* in store at the back of Nuneaton shed on 1 August 1965. She was later moved to Crewe Works for restoration and then to the Museum of Science and Industry at Birmingham. (Bryan Jeyes)

Having been delivered from Crewe, No. 46235 is waiting to have Birmingham Science Museum built around it on 10 October 1966.

In August 1965 we visited Nuneaton shed and were surprised to discover *City of Birmingham* at the back of the shed in store. Bereft of nameplates, she was filthy dirty and awaiting a visit to Crewe which came shortly afterwards. By October 1966 she had been immaculately restored and was transported to her new home in Birmingham, where a museum was built around her. She was sited where she could move forward a few feet with some rather unsynchronised sound effects playing as she was pulled along a very short length of track.

The next time I saw a Duchess was in the 1970s while passing through Minehead. No. 6229 *Duchess of Hamilton* looked rather forlorn on a short length of track on display at Butlins. Her paint was already fading – how wonderful that she was eventually restored to working order in BR Crimson Lake, surely the best colour scheme for these fine engines. In 1982 and 1983 I had a couple of trips behind her and it was a real privilege to ride behind a red Duchess once again. Sadly she has now been restored as a static exhibit with the very ugly LMS streamlining (which to some extent is rescued by a very fine livery accentuating the engine's length). Happily, we still have *Duchess of Sutherland* at work.

All that remains of Duchess No. 46256 – here we have a low-key display of nameplates from a very interesting set of Pacific engines at Clapham Museum on 15 February 1966. At the top is No. 46256, with A2 No. 60537 below it. Restored and unrestored West Country Class nameplates complete the set, from 34011 and 34016 respectively. Note the delivery tags still in place.

Even in June 1962, when I took this photo, you could expect a steady stream of Duchess-headed expresses on the West Coast Main Line. Here we have red-painted No. 46256 *Sir William A. Stanier FRS* at Leighton Buzzard heading north on 6 June 1962.

Last Rites – The Bedford Branch

In 1872 the Midland Railway decided to gain access to the London & North Western Railway stronghold of Northampton. So they built a switchback route from Bedford with its own impressive station in Northampton and three intermediate ports of call along the line. By the late 1950s its future was looking precarious and in 1962 the inevitable happened. Passenger services were withdrawn after unsuccessful experiments with both diesel rail buses and multiple units; freight services over most of the line were axed in 1964, leaving just a short section from Northampton to Piddington where there was a military camp.

It says something about the way railways were closed in those days that for a couple of years after closure, you could peer through the dusty windows at Piddington station and see the ticket office neatly ordered with lots of tickets in racks and staff caps on hooks, as though everyone had just taken half an hour off for a tea break. It was not until 1967 that someone in a BR Property Board office somewhere noticed that the line still existed, and decided to call in the demolition men to recover some assets. Considering the haste with which some railways were lifted, this line did well to hang on for so long.

Early in 1967 they started removing the track, commencing at the Bedford end. I was a close witness to this operation, so was able to see the devastation that the salvage workers wrought. Signals were felled, signal boxes smashed up, footbridges carved into chunks by oxy-acetylene torch; tracks were lifted and even the ballast was hauled away. When about a third of the line had been removed and I had taken a few photographs of the twice weekly demolition trains, I called the BR London Midland Region Press Office and asked if I could ride on one of the demolition trains. This was quickly agreed, as I was an accredited journalist about to write a story for my newspaper. I was instructed to present myself at Northampton station a few days later, which was a sunny day in March 1967. After a short while a pair of BR/Sulzer Type 2 engines (Class 24) arrived in platform one and I was invited aboard. We quickly set off to collect the empty wagons on which would be loaded materials recovered from demolishing the railway. The pair of diesels was separated and the second locomotive (No. D5058) was left to follow us as a light engine. Our engine was D5009. I remember the driver being very friendly and most amused by my wanting to travel on the train.

'No murders happening today to keep you busy?' he joked.

'I just thought it would make an interesting story,' I replied.

'Well, it's a nice job for us – easy and lots of hanging around. But don't print that!'

Having stopped at Piddington station with a demolition train, No. D5006 runs round its train prior to propelling it to Olney station for loading. The small signal controls access to the extensive tracks of a very secretive military area in Salcey Forest that did not appear on Ordnance Survey maps. Occasionally, in earlier days, a small shunter would appear from the siding, which in this view still shows signs of use. In fact after the Northampton–Bedford line was lifted, a connection from Northampton to here was retained. 31 March 1967.

Here on 31 March 1967 we see Sulzer No. D5006 (Class 24) passing through Piddington station on the closed Northampton–Bedford line. The engine ran round its train and then pushed it east to Olney where demolition of the station and the railway was taking place. A very melancholy duty.

Another shot of D5006 having arrived at Piddington with a demolition train on 31 March 1967. It looks as though it has received a cab repaint – it was apparently in Derby Works at the beginning of the year. The signalman has arrived in his Morris 1100 specially to control the movements. D5006 will now move forward and run round its empty train, prior to propelling it to Olney for loading, where a light engine (D5008) will join it for the loaded run back to Northampton. Can it really be nearly fifty years ago?

The remaining stump of the old Bedford branch on 27 May 2012. It goes as far as Brackmills, in east Northampton, but has not been used for a long time. (Nick Evans)

Here we see the old Midland Railway engine shed and water tower at Northampton. The line to the right goes to the old St John's Street station, but was just a long siding on 22 August 1965 when I took this picture. Further to the left of me were the Wellingborough and Bedford lines heading for Bridge Street station.

The same building forty-seven years later. Once used for locomotives on services from Bedford Midland to Northampton St John's Street, the Midland Railway engine shed still survives. It is a two-road engine shed, but when I knew it in the 1960s it was being used by the engineers' department, although not as a training centre. Seen here on 27 May 2012, it may become a restaurant. (Nick Evans)

Many people would not have realised the hidden platforms of Northampton St John's Street station, terminus of the Bedford line, survived in the mid-1960s. One person who did was photographer Les Hanson, whom I met on this day. He gave me a lovely picture of a train in the station he had taken in the late 1930s, showing its overall roof. Some sources say this site was cleared in 1960 – but we know better! Only the station building was demolished. This image was captured on 22 August 1965, looking towards Bridge Street.

The jocularity in the cab rather contrasted with the grim nature of the task. We rumbled down to Far Cotton with the power unit of the locomotive throbbing away just behind the bulkhead separating the cab from the engine compartment. While we waited at Far Cotton for the road ahead, the driver took me along the narrow corridor next to the engine where it was very noisy indeed. Once back in the cab, we sat and waited ... and waited. At last around one o'clock, we got a green signal and pulled across Bridge Street level crossing, on past the power station and took the tracks to the left at Hardingstone Junction. Here the Bedford line climbed over the Northampton to Wellingborough route, by then also closed.

Our Class 24 made light work of the load, despite the hilly nature of the route. We soon arrived at Piddington station, where a signalman had driven out to operate the points in his Morris 1100. He opened up the signal box, gave us the right away plus a wave and we headed off towards the next station at Olney. Here we were greeted with a swarm of demolition men armed with a vast crane. The track beyond Olney had already been removed. Soon No. D5058 also arrived and, together with D5009, which had run round its train, the two engines coupled up at the other end of the long string of wagons, which were quickly loaded with track and scrap.

Right: The demolition men are about to start the last rites at Olney engine shed. It often housed a 4F 0-6-0, which sometimes pottered along the SMJ with freight. 17 March 1967.

Below: Wagons of recovered sleepers await our train back to Northampton. 17 March 1967.

As I wandered around taking photographs, men were knocking down signals, starting to slice up the iron footbridge and removing sidings. There seemed to be small piles of things burning all over the station site. I wandered up into the shell of the signal box, by now devoid of windows and levers. It gave me a great vista of a scene of total destruction. It was as if a meteorite had just landed. As someone who knew the line well, I found it a pretty miserable last journey. After a couple of hours, all the track and debris was loaded aboard our wagons, I joined the front engine of our pair (this time No. D5058) and we moved off towards Northampton with a much heavier load than the one we brought. I do recall the driver asking me if I wished to stop anywhere to take pictures.

'How about Ravenstone Wood Junction?' I asked. 'And maybe at Great Houghton.' In each case we pulled up and I clambered down to take a couple of pictures.

Within a few days the tracks were removed from Olney station, everything but the station building and platforms having been levelled. Over the next few weeks I continued to photograph the demolition trains until at last all the track had been removed.

It's great to know that although Olney station was demolished, the other two, Turvey and Piddington, still survive, the latter owned by Norman Oldfield, who has done a wonderful job of preserving it, even rebuilding the main platform and importing an old Coronation Scot coach, latterly in departmental service. Inside what is now a charming house, you are never in any doubt that this was once a railway station, as Norman has skilfully made features from its heritage. He has ambitious plans to do more. It's a noble act that allows us to gain a flavour of what this interesting branch and its attractive stations were like. I see Norman now and then and every time I visit there are more improvements. Long may it continue.

Waiting to leave Olney station with the detritus that was once a handsome railway station and yard are Sulzer diesels Nos D5009/D5005 on 23 March 1967. They are standing well to the Northampton end of the station with a demolition special. The Down line has already been removed.

Here we are, just west of Olney station and the two Sulzer diesels working the demolition train are running round their train. This was the day I joined the crew for this working, 17 March 1967 (thanks to British Railways for my unforgettable ride).

I suppose this is the sort of picture that seemed boring at the time, but forty-five years later is quite interesting. It shows the Northampton to Bedford railway running through Great Houghton on 10 April 1967. Now it is just a long-lost memory.

All that's left of Olney signal box on 23 March 1967. A week earlier I had been taking photographs from it.

Olney Station, Buckinghamshire, where the supports of the footbridge have been cut into sections and are being loaded in the demolition train to be towed away for scrap. An old piece of telegraph pole acts as a temporary buffer stop. It's a desolate scene. 23 March 1967.

Olney station. It looks like a Standard Vanguard and a VW Beetle are in residence. Taken on 17 March 1967, this picture disguises the devastation taking place on the platform side of the building.

Nothing exemplifies last rites more than the demolition of a much-loved railway, in this case from Northampton to Bedford. Here we see Type 2 diesel No. D5059 at Hardingstone Crossing, Northampton. This section of track was shared by the Wellingborough and Bedford lines once St John's Street station had closed. No. D5059 and its sister No. D5057 (which followed light engine and then helped to haul the loaded train back to Northampton) were among the regular engines. The day is a wet 10 April 1967. On 17 March I had ridden on the train to Olney and back in the cab. The missing signal arm is for the Wellingborough line.

Olney station in March 1967 with a demolition train in the platform. Work on tearing down the infrastructure here had just started.

As if a meteorite had just landed – Olney station in March 1967.

Apart from some scruffiness and the removal of lamps and name boards, Piddington looks, on 17 March 1967, very much as it did when the final passenger train ran five years earlier. Even the station porter's hat was hanging on a peg in the office, clearly visible through a dusty window. The building still stands today. Notice the huge chimneys. Passengers crossed the line by a wooden crossing – there was no footbridge. Piddington village was a long way away; you went through both Horton and Hackleton before reaching it!

The one that got away – Piddington station in 2015, with the demolished platform rebuilt and even a carriage on site. This, believe it or not, is the kitchen car from the Coronation Scot streamlined train. It was built by the Gloucester Railway Carriage & Wagon Co. in 1937 and then rebuilt at Wolverton as an inspection saloon. Eventually it was sold to a new owner who converted it to a camping coach. Now it has been moved to Northamptonshire for a new life. Inside it is beautifully fitted out, but retains much of the original panelling and other details from its life on the Coronation Scot. Thanks to Norman Oldfield for letting me see this wonderful and very historic vehicle. It is in good hands.

Last Rites – 'Non League Lines'

Imagine Britain's railways as the Football League. In the Premier League you have the expresses speeding along on four track main lines. Three lower divisions comprise cross-country routes, branch lines and lastly shunting yards. Yet there is a world of activity going on below that, all those teams that play in local leagues or just people having fun on a Saturday afternoon kicking a ball about in the local park. The railways had an equivalent for that – the hundreds of miles of industrial railways that went about their daily business largely unseen by the public.

Back in the 1950s this 'subculture' was enormous. There were coal mines, all kinds of industrial plants, power stations, steel works and, in my territory, dozens of ironstone quarries.

A wide band of ironstone runs through much of the East Midlands, stretching from around Banbury through Northamptonshire, Leicestershire and into Lincolnshire. Eric Tonks lists just under 160 quarries in his seminal eight-part work *The Ironstone Quarries of the Midlands*, but the situation is complicated, as sometimes new quarries were opened right next to where old ones had closed. One thing we can say for sure is that there were a lot, many of them still busy in the 1960s.

On 21 September 1965 this ironstone engine passed through Northampton on its way to Cohen's at Cransley for scrapping. It looks in quite good condition, having been replaced by a diesel.

At George Cohen's yard at Cransley, Northants, on 11 December 1969 is this Western Region shunter from 1948, No. 15101. This was a Great Western version of the standard LMS shunter. Stewarts and Lloyds 0-6-0ST No. 39 is also awaiting its fate. Even diesels were not safe from the scrap man.

On 5 August 1965, this industrial 0-4-0ST with nameplates removed was in store near the BR depot at Canklow, Sheffield. She is probably an Andrew Barclay engine that came from a Stewart & Lloyds plant in the area, on its way for scrap.

The last hours of an attractive little Oxfordshire Ironstone 0-4-0ST as it is reduced to scrap at Cransley on 25 September 1965. A 9F 2-10-0 awaits its turn in the background. (Bryan Jeyes)

It's getting near the end for 0-6-0ST *Pitsford*, which is in her shed at Pitsford Quarries on 4 February 1966. There is just enough track left for her to run down to the BR exchange sidings.

Stewarts & Lloyds 0-6-0T No. 3 from Glendon Quarries standing at Cransley scrapyard – a big engine from the 'little league.' Seen on 11 December 1969, when I was told it had been sold for preservation as it was in excellent condition. They covered the chimney and sheeted over the cab to protect the engine. But, eventually, salvation did not happen and she was scrapped.

Paying my last respects to some ironstone quarries, I found myself at Cranford Quarry where this old Avonside engine named *Stamford*, stripped of its nameplates, silently awaited its fate. Happily it was not scrapped. It was rescued, and you can see it – and the adjacent dump truck – at Rocks by Rail museum in Rutland.

If you drove through the countryside in these counties during that period, the sight of a massive crane jib sticking out of a distant field was quite common. These huge excavators shovelled the ironstone out of the ground, filling wagons that were sent on a rickety (and temporary) railway to connect with British Railways, usually through a branch or cross-country route. Because the area of excavation was always moving, the lightly laid tracks had to move too. The quarry managers were not keen on letting schoolboys ('some kids' like myself) enter the actual working quarry, but we were always welcome to take pictures or wander around the other areas.

Often these lines had fierce gradients. You didn't need to go to the Lickey Incline to see a locomotive being worked flat out. Just pop along to a local quarry and watch a tiny 0-6-0 tank engine tug three or four fully loaded iron ore tippler wagons out of a quarry and you'll get all the action you need. There was a huge variety of locomotives, many of them built by industrial engine specialists like Avonside, Manning Wardle, Hunslet and others. Most had outside cylinders for easy maintenance and saddle tanks were the norm. Diesels were almost unheard of in our area, although a few, including some ex-BR engines, appeared further north. New industrial steam locomotives were still being delivered in the late 1950s. I remember looking at a builder's plate on the Barclay 0-4-0ST *Blisworth No. 1* during my first visit to the nearby Blisworth quarry in 1964. Amazingly this filthy dirty, ancient-looking engine was less than ten years old. I wondered if it had ever been cleaned since that day in 1955 when it appeared brand new at Blisworth.

A strange quarry system about to close – here we have a train emerging from the tunnel at Irthlingborough on 1 October 1966. Notice the strange battery electric locomotive. This was an open day working.

This sturdy little 0-4-0ST, *Blisworth No. 1*, was one of the regular engines right to the end at Blisworth Mines, Northamptonshire, where she is seen in April 1967. She was cut up for scrap when the quarry closed a few months later.

Holwell No. 14, an 0-6-0ST, at New Bradwell station on the Wolverton–Newport Pagnell branch. She was brought from Glendon Quarries near Corby for cutting up. She is seen here awaiting her fate on 28 May 1966. You found scrap engines in the most unusual places.

Recorded for posterity, this engine is Barclay 0-6-0ST No. 84 from Glendon Quarries, awaiting cutting up at New Bradwell station on 28 May 1966.

The Peckett 0-4-0ST *Henry Cort* at Irthlingborough quarry on 1 October 1966, a year after closure and before it was saved for preservation. She was donated to the Foxfield Railway for preservation.

Like many quarries, Blisworth owned a ramshackle set of engines, a couple of which had been handed on from South Wales. It also had most of the normal features of such lines. It connected through some exchange sidings with the SMJ line near Blisworth. It had one of those massive excavators with a giant boom, a corrugated-looking cab area and a confusion of cables and wires to swing the shovel and scoop the ore out of the ground. I seem to recall a smaller machine was also there. If you looked around you, it was plain to see how the countryside was actually lower than the roads and paths. All this land had been stripped of its iron ore, leaving a kind of two-tier landscape that was a hallmark of ironstone lines.

I returned many years later to find the engine shed still there, but with the landscape having been restored and all the cuttings filled in, it was very hard to picture trains running through it. The Blisworth Quarries were among the last in our area to survive. Along with Lamport, Pitsford, Irchester and the narrow gauge system at Finedon, Blisworth clung on, just a few wagons of brightly coloured iron ore being moved down to the nearby station each week for onward transportation to the steelworks.

For many years it was good business for British Railways and trains of iron ore were a very common sight in the East Midlands. Yet almost overnight, the whole industry seemed to disappear. In the early 1960s there were quarries busy throughout Northamptonshire. By 1970 they had all gone. Demand for steel was declining and the iron ore quarrying business naturally mirrored this trend. In fact the movement of iron ore, especially to South Wales, had actually created certain local railways.

On 11 April 1967 at Blisworth Mines, Northamptonshire, the engines in steam are *Ettrick* and *Siemens*. *Ettrick*, seen here, was a Hawthorn Leslie product built in 1928. She had been given a quick coat of cheap pale blue paint over her previous handsome green in 1965. It did nothing for her looks, but *Ettrick* was always my favorite of the Blisworth stud. I've no idea about her odd name, except that there is a place on the Scottish borders named Ettrick. She was sold for preservation but eventually was cut up.

I never actually saw this engine, *No. 49*, in steam at Blisworth, although it must have run because sometimes it was in the shed, sometimes outside. She was built by Hunslet in 1940 and was always known by us as the 'Ebbw Vale tank.' So it may have come to Blisworth from South Wales with *Siemens*. Here she is outside the shed in 1966.

Here we are at the South Durham system of quarries at Irchester, Northamptonshire. The Hawthorn Leslie 0-4-0ST *Holwell No. 30* is coming uphill near Wollaston with a fully loaded train of iron ore on 10 February 1968. She was cut up nearby at the Cransley yard of George Cohen the following year (one of three sent there) after the system closed in June 1969.

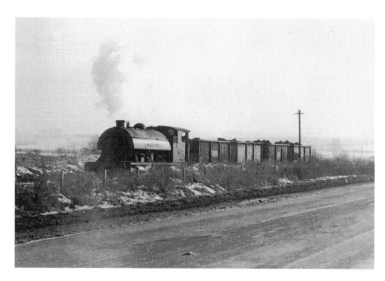

At Cransley scrapyard, Kettering, on 26 September 1965 was a batch of engines from the Oxfordshire Ironstone Co. This diesel engine had been purchased in 1955 but was unsuccessful and little used. It is sandwiched between some of the same quarry's steam locomotives.

This Fowler diesel locomotive was in quite good condition but its future looked bleak. It was standing in the yard at Brackley Town station on 9 April 1966 among a whole host of items that appeared to be for auction.

Here is one of several industrial diesels standing in Brackley station goods yard on 9 April 1966 awaiting disposal. This one was in particularly poor condition. I know nothing of its history, but in those days you could find odd locomotives almost anywhere, often awaiting scrap.

What a little gem we found here among the Fowler diesels in Brackley Town station yard on 9 April 1966. This tiny narrow gauge 0-6-0ST with an immense chimney is named *Mesozoic*. I'm not sure what it was doing at Brackley, but it had served for many years at Kay and Co.'s cement works near Southam (later Rugby Portland Cement). It was built in 1913 and is now at a narrow gauge railway project in Herefordshire, but rather derelict, I gather.

Once an everyday scene at countless ironstone quarries throughout Northamptonshire, this is the main line side of Lamport Quarry. A Brush Type 4 diesel is about to leave towards Market Harborough with rich, red ironstone; empty wagons have been left for the next train on 6 April 1966.

Decline and Fall

Our last visit to Blisworth was a few weeks before closure, yet two locomotives were still needed for the work. One hauled the loaded wagons up to the engine shed sidings, while a second locomotive was busy handling traffic between the sidings and the truncated remains of the old Blisworth to Towcester SMJ line. Pulling the empties uphill from the SMJ was quite a task and these trains usually had an ancient Midland Railway brake van attached, perhaps to cope with a 'runaway'. The quarry was actually closed for many years. It then reopened in 1955 and a bright long-term future was forecast at the time for the industry. It was not to be. Sadly, all the engines from Blisworth were cut up for scrap, despite an ill-fated attempt to preserve *Ettrick*.

At around the same time we also visited Lamport Quarries on several occasions. But this pit, with its well-cleaned engines, had almost had its day. One day we arrived a bit late to see operations, but the driver cheerfully moved *Lamport No. 3* out of the shed for us to photograph. Lamport also possessed a diesel, an unloved Fowler 0-4-0 which the driver said 'couldn't pull the skin off a rice pudding.' Latterly it was left outside while the three steam engines, including one that had not run for some time, were kept inside the shed. *Lamport No. 3* is still with us at the Battlefield Railway in Leicestershire, and *Robert* had a starring Olympic role when it was refurbished and put on display at Stratford in London for the games in 2012.

Deep underneath that coat of grime is green paint! Here we see *Blisworth No. 1* ready to head down to the quarry with empties for filling. *Siemens* was running the route down to the exchange sidings on the Blisworth–Towcester line on 5 April 1966. Both engines were cut up for scrap.

Above: Heading light down to the quarry, *Blisworth No. 1* trundles along to collect some full wagons. The dragline and crane can be seen on the skyline, a familiar part of the East Midlands landscape. As usual, there is someone hanging on the footsteps catching a ride (April 5 1966).

Right: It's 11 April 1967 and time is running out for steam in Northamptonshire. Blisworth Mines, run by Richard Thomas Baldwins, would close in September 1967, but here we have the 0-4-0ST *Siemens* blasting uphill pushing six empties and towing a battered Midland Railway brake van. From this point she will coast down to the quarry. Steam action survives – just.

Left: *Siemens* has now breasted the summit under a road bridge and can coast downhill to the engine shed and quarry. This picture gives a better view of the old brake van. The line had steep gradients, so maybe it offered extra braking assistance. There was a guy inside the van. The track was well maintained right to the end on this section. Where did the engine's odd name come from? Well, the German multinational company Siemens built a steel plant at Landore in South Wales and, as this engine was built at Ebbw Vale Iron Works in 1909, it seems likely that she got her name because the ironworks were at one time owned by Siemens UK. She ended up being scrapped a few months after this picture was taken.

Below: When I arrived at Lamport Quarry shed on 6 April 1966, the driver had just put *Lamport No. 3* away for the night, but he obligingly drove it out again so I could get some pictures. Quarry lines were like that.

Right: In her shed at Lamport on 11 April 1967 is 0-6-0ST *Lamport No. 2*. The engines were painted mid-green with black lining edged in red and yellow, but earlier had been dark green with the black lining edged in white, if I remember correctly. *Robert*, in front, was saved but *Lamport No. 2* was scrapped.

Below: Lamport ironstone mines, Northamptonshire, on April 6 1966 with 0-4-0 diesel *Douglas* outside the shed. On this day steam engines were in use – in fact *Douglas* was seldom at work when I visited. She was eventually scrapped.

On April 11 1967, *Lamport No. 3* rests in her dilapidated shed waiting for a decision on her future. Happily, things turned out okay and both this engine and *Robert* were saved. I suppose the other engine, *Lamport No. 2*, felt the hot torch.

An old favourite from Lamport Mines now at work on the Battlefield Line in Leicestershire. Here is *Lamport No. 3* in October 1983 at Market Bosworth station.

A view towards the offices and engine shed at Pitsford Quarry, with the main Northampton–Market Harborough line in the background. Here, on 16 February 1966, work has started in track lifting and I bet many newer residents of the village have no idea that a quarry railway was once on their doorstep.

The quarry at Pitsford, just north of Northampton, closed in 1965. Both of the locomotives finally in use, *Pitsford* and *No. 65*, remained on short lengths of track after the closure and we were quite apprehensive about their future. *Pitsford* was still in its shed, and you could wander over, push back the doors and take photographs of her. Despite this, the engine retained its nameplates and there was no vandalism. Eventually we heard it was being preserved and a few people congregated to watch it set off under its own power on 25 June 1966 along the Northampton to Market Harborough Railway for a new life. She is now at the Elsecar Heritage Railway in South Yorkshire, carrying the name *Earl Fitzwilliam*, all trace of her humble ancestry having been sadly removed, with a dark red livery replacing her original 'ironstone green.'

What about *No. 65*? This engine spent about two years being overhauled in the open at Pitsford, before being moved to a quarry at Crosby for further service. It, too, has been preserved, and has recently spent many years giving service on the Derwent Valley Light Railway. Unfortunately in 1996 its appearance was ruined when it was rebuilt as a side tank with a very ugly cab.

Industrial railways seldom had last days. But the metre gauge ironstone line at Wellingborough Quarries went out with a very special event, with two of the engines spotlessly cleaned for the day and trains full of enthusiasts in little skip wagons. I managed to persuade my news editor that this was an event worth covering. It was a Saturday and that normally meant a working day for me, but a few hours watching trains did not seem too arduous. I breezed over to the quarry in my little Fiat 600 to join the fun. This was another of those 'last days' that seemed to be something of a celebration. In fact Wellingborough Quarries had a long history and much of the hillside had been quarried over the years. There was also a mine which was operating for that special day and showing another, rarer way of extracting ore.

Pitsford standing in the exchange sidings at Pitsford quarry on 24 June 1966. Next day she headed north, bunker first, up the Market Harborough line in steam, possibly the last engine to work in steam in the Northampton area on BR metals.

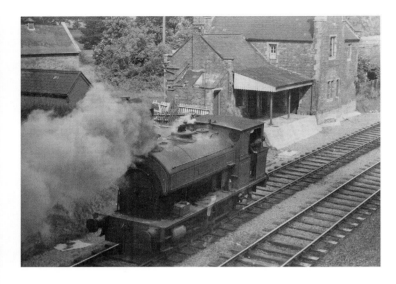

Pitsford leaves its home and is seen here passing through Pitsford and Brampton station on 25 June 1966.

Nothing but the best for those overhauling 0-6-0ST *No. 65* at Pitsford Quarry. Here on 16 February 1965, the boiler has been fitted and she will leave this closed quarry for a new life.

The parts of *No. 65* are strewn around at Pitsford, with one man carrying out the overhaul on 4 February 1966 as she prepares for a new life. In fact it was June 1966 before she was ready to steam again. In those days you could leave bits of the engine all over the place and they would not get stolen.

After a very long time being overhauled in the open (about two years), *No. 65* has at last been reassembled, as seen here on 24 June 1966 ready for further service. This was my final visit to Pitsford as both *No. 65* and *Pitsford* were ready to head to pastures new. This is a nice looking Hudswell Clarke tank engine with a usefully short wheelbase and it looks quite powerful. She is No. 1631 of 1929. The overhaul clearly did not include a repaint.

Last day of the metre gauge system at Wellingborough on 1 October 1966. Here we see No. 85 in the quarry area. It was always difficult to know whether to travel on the train or photograph it on these occasions. On this one, as at the last day of the Cromford and High Peak, the pictures won out. The chimney extension carried a spark arrester. These were beefy engines and hearing one blasting uphill from the exchange sidings was a rare treat.

Holwell No. 30 heading for Wellingborough London Road with a load of iron ore. The date is 7 December 1967. She is a Hawthorne Leslie-built 0-4-0ST and has a decent load in tow.

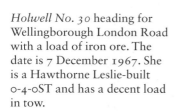

Here we are at Sidegate Lane quarry near Wellingborough. No. 87 was perfectly turned out for its last day of proper work. Seen at the quarry is the train and a Ruston Bucyrus dragline in the background. 1 October 1966.

Peckett metre gauge engine Nos 85 and 87 reverse downhill towards the main line with a last day special at Wellingborough Quarries.

The very last ironstone line in the Northampton area was at Irchester, where the final rites were not performed until 1969. If you drove along the road between Wellingborough and Olney, you would notice a single track railway running parallel with the highway, with rather ramshackle fencing. Here you could witness impressive action on the last quarry line in the Northampton area. The two engines usually at work were *Holwell No. 30* and *Carmarthen*. Both were refugees from other quarries, as their names suggest, and both were dispatched to a local scrapyard in 1969 on closure of the system, but a couple of the many locomotives that operated at Irchester made it into preservation. When Irchester Quarry closed in late 1969, it was the end of an era.

In early 1967 I received a phone call while working at my desk at the *Chronicle and Echo*. A chap on the end of the phone had noticed I had written some stories about railways.

'Would you be interested in coming and seeing a steam engine?' I was asked. There was clearly only one answer to that and I was given an address in a back street in west Northampton. I arrived outside an unprepossessing-looking old brick building and was warmly greeted. We walked into a workshop through a door and standing there was a Hunslet 0-6-0 saddle tank, looking huge in a fairly compact building.

'We are overhauling it – it's from Nassington quarries out near Corby,' I was told. I wish I could remember more about it or could find the cutting of the article I wrote, but this one has escaped me. However, I was given the workshop manual for the locomotive which I still have on my bookshelf today. Its grubby, oily pages tell of a book well used. I never heard of another engine being overhauled here (or anywhere else in Northampton) and, indeed, this company had tendered for the work and were a bit surprised to get the job. The engine looked splendid as it was being prepared to return to its working home, although they did not paint it.

Many people may think that the last working steam engines in the Northampton area were based at Irchester Quarries. But as you can see here, steam survived in the town itself in 1973. Here is one of the locomotives at Northampton Power Station (or Nunn Mills Power Station), a Bagnall 0-4-0ST saddle tank, seen busy on 28 April 1973. There was a link from the power station to the Northampton–Wellingborough line near Hardingstone Junction.

The cooling towers at Northampton Power Station loom over the plant's fireless locomotive, with a Peckett behind. On this day she was not in use, but when I did see her running she was the only fireless engine I ever saw working. Notice the Walschaerts valve gear and the unusual arrangement of the cylinders. It's as though someone put the accumulator/boiler unit and cab on the wrong way round. An engine like this made a lot of sense at a power station, with all its free hot water, but its endurance was quite short and it was less powerful than the other engines. I am told this engine was built by Hawthorn Leslie, but Andrew Barclay were the main builders of these engines in the UK. Most had square cab windows. 16 March 1973.

Here we see all three engines at Northampton Power Station on 30 March 1973. On the left is the Bagnall, centre is the Peckett and right is the fireless. On this wet day all three were in steam. They are surrounded by the industrial archaeology of a busy power generation plant.

Above: On 28 April 1973 Northampton Power Station held an open day, but it was not widely advertised and very few people turned up. Here we see the fireless and the Peckett at work, having been given an extra burnish. The fireless engine is essentially a very heavily insulated container that is filled with superheated water to create the steam. I wonder if this engine was eventually scrapped. Notice the motley collection of coal wagons.

Right: Northampton Power Station's Bagnall 0-4-0ST is seen here busy shunting on March 16 1973. Judging by the marks on the tank, at some stage in its life this engine carried a name. I have often wondered what happened to these three carefully maintained engines, as we were well into the preservation era, but at this time I left the Northampton area.

Cherwell – Saved Twice From Scrap

I find industrial railways and their locomotives surprisingly interesting. With their variety of liveries and neat outlines, they were just as attractive in their way as the main line heroes of more obvious appeal. When we were walking the SMJ, we came across Byfield Ironstone Mines, by then closed and the track lifted. But standing on a short length of rails was the 0-6-0 saddle tank *Cherwell*, isolated and facing an uncertain future.

Happily, she evaded the cutter's torch. Daventry Borough Council acquired her and transported the engine to New Street Recreation Ground and, of course, I had to see her. All the fittings had been removed and anything moveable had been welded up. Still, she was extant for a new generation of admirers to see – and for children to play on. It seemed a somewhat ignominious fate, but more recently she has been rescued again and taken to Rushden in Northamptonshire, where a project to restore part of the long-closed line from Wellingborough to Higham Ferrers is under way.

She looks so sad and clearly a very major overhaul will be needed to return her to operating condition. But who would dare to predict that *Cherwell* will never grace a Northampton railway in steam once again?

The engine shed at Byfield Mines on 23 June 1966. The quarries had closed the previous year and nature is already starting to take over. Now it is hard to find anything that suggests a railway once ran here.

I was at Loughborough Central on 14 July 1974 in the early days of the revived Great Central Railway. Like many early preservation schemes, industrial engines were found to be very useful. Here we see an 0-6-0ST, *Littleton No. 5*, which had arrived at the Great Central on 25 October the previous year. It was built by Manning Wardle and worked at a colliery near Cannock. I gather this engine is now at the Avon Valley Railway. Notice the coach gangway board lettered MLST (Main Line Steam Trust, the origins of the Great Central) ... and the miniature railway. Heritage lines quickly outgrew these industrial survivors.

Industrial engines that escaped cutting up now have a novelty value on the busier preserved lines, like this sturdy 0-6-0T *Nunlow* at the Keighley & Worth Valley Railway. It is here looking immaculate on 10 October 2014. In its working days it was used at a cement works in Derbyshire and I bet it never looked like this.

Last Rites – Special Trains

Sometimes a railway enthusiast's first journey over a line was also the last. This happened to me on several occasions. Such an event was the Somerset and Dorset rail tour on 2 January 1966. The closure of this fascinating line was big news, as it was a much-loved route to which certain brilliant photographers had given a very high profile. With all that single track and some very steep gradients, it must have been an operating nightmare, especially as it was steam-operated right to the end. On summer Saturdays it carried a huge volume of traffic from the Midlands and the North heading for the south coast resorts around Bournemouth. Bryan and I presented ourselves at Waterloo station, where Merchant Navy 4-6-2 No. 35011 *General Steam Navigation* was ready to whisk us to Bournemouth. Here light Pacific No. 34015 *Exmouth* and a Class U 2-6-0 took over for the run to Bath. This was a much more melancholy event than some farewell trips (although a late stay of execution meant that this was not the advertised last day after all). I recall everyone piling out of the train at Evercreech Junction to take pictures in a scene which would cause apoplexy to today's world of hi-vis jackets and bureaucrats believing nobody has any common sense. Amazingly, nobody died.

The Somerset and Dorset rail tour, Evercreech Junction, on 2 January 1966. Both engines, a U class and a West Country 4-6-2, had been cleaned for the occasion.

At Bath Green Park a Stanier 2-8-0 took over for the run to Bristol and Highbridge, with the run back to Templecombe in the hands of a pair of Ivatt 2-6-2Ts. The Merchant Navy had made its way to Templecombe in the meantime, so it could haul us back to Waterloo. What a great day out.

Some of the local 'farewell' specials were just as interesting. On 3 July 1965 the Locomotive Club of Great Britain ran a tour around closed (or threatened) lines in Northamptonshire, hauled by 2-6-0 No. 78022, which had been brought from Leicester for the occasion. Starting and finishing at Kettering, it gave us a last chance to traverse some old favourite lines aboard the undignified, but fascinating, vantage point of a row of brake vans. Possibly the most amazing part of the trip, and the reason for using brake vans, was an attempt to cover the old Loddington branch, a mineral line which led to a quarry that was closed. The track was in a very poor condition, but had been left *in situ* in case the quarry was needed at some time in the future. The Standard 2-6-0 set off from Kettering station propelling the twelve brake vans, running steeply downhill towards the bridge under the A43 road from Northampton to Kettering and through the site of Cransley ironworks, by then a scrapyard. At once the crew of No. 78028 piled on the pressure and we slammed uphill, but the gradient and the load were too much. No. 78028 stalled on the bank in a location which appeared to be the middle of a field. We reversed back to the level track at Cransley and the determined crew had another go. It was a plucky attempt, but she still couldn't quite get us to the top. So we all piled out and walked. What a wonderful tour that was.

The last train from Bletchley to Oxford was run in vastly different circumstances. Slated for closure by Beeching, and fiercely opposed, there was an air of angry resignation among the participants as the diesel multiple unit headed to Oxford and back. I recall a few detonators going off somewhere, but it was as if British Rail couldn't wait to eliminate an irritating child from the family. On arrival at Bletchley we were all turfed off the platform by a zealous member of the station staff.

Ironically, the line is now being restored to passenger use as part of a new east–west artery.

This is the almost unknown mineral branch from Kettering to Loddington. Here, No. 78028 is in sylvan surroundings with a rail tour, having stalled trying to push twelve brake vans up the last part of the bank. It was a good effort by the game crew of a very small engine on 3 July 1965.

On 3 July 1965, this LCGB special toured branch lines around Northampton, starting and ending at Kettering. Motive power was Standard Class 2 2-6-0 No. 78028 from Leicester, in unlined black. The first port of call was Higham Ferrers, where the train has just arrived, a station closed to passengers some six years earlier.

Last rites at Southampton as both station and engines here have only a couple of years to survive. Two USA class 0-6-0Ts, Nos 30073 and 30069, built in America, are at Southampton Terminus. They made a good, if leisurely, job of hauling a Home Counties special train to Eastleigh on 6 December 1964. It's not often a USA gets a Class 1 job.

Valediction

My photographic collection includes some 300 black and white shots, mainly taken when I was a penniless student, so every photograph was financially precious. I seem to recall my pocket money was about 2s 6d a week – 12.5p today! That would buy you some film, but not the processing and prints. A role of Kodachrome colour transparency film, including processing, was over £2. Once I started work, I moved up a gear and took around 2,000 colour pictures between 1965 and 1985.

The end of steam was the major event in the railway life of my generation of enthusiasts, but the decline of the railways continued after that as more lines were lifted, rationalised and left to become derelict.

A Bagnall locomotive, this time in working order. It is *Cranford No. 2,* seen at Cranford Quarry in June 1966. This was another engine to escape the great cull of ironstone quarry engines in the mid-1960s, although its early preservation existence was precarious.

Cranford No. 2 again, this time in February 1970 when this engine was unloaded at Overstone Solarium, near Northampton, with a view to using it for tourist trains around the park. The venture did not last long. I seem to remember there was an accident of some kind which canned the project. It happily ended up at the Rocks by Rail Museum.

When visiting my local heritage line, the Keighley & Worth Valley Railway, or watching a steam special come past, it's not hard to flash back to those halcyon days. The smell, the whirling coupling rods, the driver as master of his engine – it's all there. Only this time there is no timetable of destruction. Long may it all survive.

Bibliography

Allen, Cecil, *The ABC of British Locomotives Combined Volume* (London: Ian Allan Ltd, 1948).

The ABC of British Railways Locomotives Combined Volume (London: Ian Allan Ltd, 1959).

The ABC of British Railways Locomotives Combined Volume (London: Ian Allan Ltd, 1962).

The ABC of British Railways Locomotives Combined Volume (London: Ian Allan Ltd, 1964).

ABC British Rail Steam Locomotives (London: Ian Allan, 1965).

Antes, R., *Sectional Maps of British Railways as at January 1982* (London: Ian Allan Ltd, 1982).

Bulleid, H. A. V., *Master Builders of Steam* (London: Ian Allan Ltd, 1963).

Casserley, H. C., *Historic Steam Locomotive Pocketbook* (London: Batsford, 1960).

Casserley, H. C., *Steam Locomotives of British Railways* (Feltham: Hamlyn, 1973).

Derry, Richard, *The Book of the Britannia Pacifics* (Clophill: Irwell Press Ltd, 2004).

Dunn, J. M., *The Stratford-upon-Avon & Midland Junction Railway* (South Godstone: The Oakwood Press, 1952).

Dunn, J. M., *The Stratford-upon-Avon & Midland Junction Railway, Revised Edition* (South Godstone: The Oakwood Press, 1952).

Gilbert, P. T., *British Railways Standard Steam Locomotives Volume One – Background to Standardisation and the Pacific Classes* (Bristol: The Railway Correspondence and Travel Society, 1994).

Irons, R. and Jenkins, S. C., *Woodford Halse: A Railway Community* (Usk: The Oakwood Press, 1999).

Jordan, Arthur, *The Stratford-upon-Avon & Midland Junction Railway* (Oxford: Oxford Publishing Company, 1982).

Mitchell, Vic and Keith Smith, *Midland Main Lines – Aylesbury to Rugby* (Midhurst: Middleton Press, 2006).

Onley, Graham, *British Railways in Colour – Northampton and Beyond* (Clophill: Irwell Press, 2003).

Tonks, Eric, *The Ironstone Quarries of the Midlands, Part I, Introduction* (Cheltenham: Runpast Publishing, 1988).

Tonks, Eric, *The Ironstone Quarries of the Midlands, Part III, The Northampton Area* (Cheltenham: Runpast Publishing, 1989).

Tonks, Eric, *The Ironstone Quarries of the Midlands, Part IV, The Wellingborough Area* (Cheltenham: Runpast Publishing, 1990).

Walford, John and Paul Harrison, *British Railways Standard Steam Locomotives Volume Four – the 9F 2-10-0 Class* (Bristol: The Railway Correspondence and Travel Society, 2008).

Walker, Colin, *Main Line Lament* (Oxford: The Oxford Publishing Company, 1973).